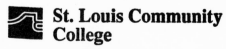

Understanding
Things Fall Apart:
Selected Essays and Criticism

Understanding
Things Fall Apart:
Selected Essays and Criticism

edited by

Solomon O. Iyasere, Ph.D.

The Whitston Publishing Company
Troy, New York
1998

For my wife

Marla Mudar Iyasere

A kindred soul.

Contents

Acknowledgments

"The Mouth with Which to Tell Their Sufferings: The Role of Narrator and Reader in Achebe's *Things Fall Apart*" by Angela Smith in *Commonwealth Essays and Studies*, 11.1 (Autumn 1988); published by the Faculté des Langues, Université de Bourgogne, Dijon, France. Reprinted with permission.

"The Search for Values Theme in Chinua Achebe's Novel, *Things Fall Apart*: A Crisis of the Soul" by Willene P. Taylor is reprinted by permission of *Griot: Official Journal of the Southern Conference on Afro-American Studies*.

"Rhythm and Narrative Methods in Achebe's *Things Fall Apart*" by B. Eugene McCarthy in *Novel* 18.3 (Spring 1985). © 1985 Novel Corp. Reprinted with permission.

"Narrative Techniques in *Things Fall Apart*" by Solomon O. Iyasere is reprinted with the permission of *New Letters*.

"The Sphinx and the Rough Beast: Linguistic Struggle in Chinua Achebe's *Things Fall Apart*" by Julian N. Wasserman is reprinted by permission of Mississippi Folklore Register.

"Sophisticated Primitivism: The Syncretism of Oral and Literate Modes in Achebe's *Things Fall Apart*" by Abdul Janmohamed is reprinted by permission of *Ariel* and the Board of Governors, The University of Calgary.

"Okonkwo's Walk: The Choreography of *Things Fall Apart*" by Russell McDougall is reprinted by permission of *World Literature Written in English* 26.1 (1986).

"Okonkwo is,
as tragic heroes often are,
a victim of the defects of his virtues"

Introduction

> ... African people did not hear of culture for the first time from Europeans; ... their societies were not mindless but frequently had a philosophy of great depth and beauty, ... they had poetry and, above all, they had dignity. It is this dignity that many African people all but lost during the colonial period and it is this that they must now regain.... The writer's duty is to help them regain it by showing them in human terms what happened to them, what they lost. —**Chinua Achebe**[1]

Things Fall Apart, black Africa's most important novel to date, is probably the most widely studied African creative work both in Africa and abroad. The novel's universal appeal has led to its being translated into more than 50 languages; since publication by Heinemann in 1958, the work has sold more than eight million copies. A film version of the novel enjoyed world-wide distribution. In 1993, Everyman's Library, the prestigious series of world classics founded in 1966, added *Things Fall Apart* to its catalog of publications.

Today, *Things Fall Apart* continues to attract a vigorous increase in readership and literary prestige in Africa, the West, and in Asia, where sales have soared. Not surprisingly, the novel appeals to readers across various disciplines; as such it is now required reading in courses in world history, world literature, and multiculturalism in universities around the world. Since writing *Things Fall Apart*, Achebe has published *No Longer at Ease*, *Arrow of God* and *A Man of the People*, among others, but none has attained the richness and the success of *Things Fall Apart*. According to Eustace Palmer, *Things Fall Apart* is unquestionably Achebe's best work. "Never again was he able to demonstrate such mastery of plot construction, such keen psychological insight, and such ability to hold his themes steadily before his mind and pursue them convincingly to a logical conclusion,"[2] Palmer writes.

As would be expected, Achebe's literary reputation rests principally on *Things Fall Apart*, a work for which he won the Margaret Wong Memorial Prize and earned international critical acclaim. It is also the principal work cited in his recent nomination for the Nobel Prize for Literature.

Things Fall Apart and Its Critics

Early reviews and commentaries on *Things Fall Apart* focused primarily on the sociological and anthropological elements of the work. The novel was hailed as a charming and curious ethnic report of quaint antique customs. The following observation by R. C. Healy (1959) is characteristic: "An authentic native document guileless and unsophisticated . . . *Things Fall Apart* is more of a chronicle of Okonkwo and his village than a full blown novel . . . there is no sense of plot or development. Things simply happen, one after the other. This is plain and unvarnished storytelling in the best primitive tradition, probably more impressive and important as an anthropological document than a novel."[3] David Hassoldt (1959) offers a similar comment, "No European ethnologist could so intimately present this medley of mores of the Ibo tribe, nor detail the intricate formalities of life in the clan. The flashbacks of the book are confusing, the narration undisciplined, but as an objective view of the Ibo customs, it is of both interest and value."[4] At first, those for whom the novel had strong appeal—and they were many— were students of sociology, anthropology, and African colonial history. This critical emphasis on the anthropological elements of the novel obscured its overall excellence as a legitimate piece of fiction. Contributions by scholars such as Ato Quayson illustrate that reading "culture" out of a novel is valuable but inadequate; such efforts must be infused with an awareness that *Things Fall Apart*, like many other novels written by Africans, possesses a richly ambivalent attitude toward its culture that can be discovered only by paying acute attention to both the reality processed and to the larger rhetorical strategies employed.[5] As I have argued elsewhere,[6] emphasis on cultural elements alone inevitably leads to misreading and misrepresentation of the significant characters and events portrayed in the text.

The novel suffered a similar fate in the hands of literary critics, especially those who examined the work from only a Eurocentric point of view. This approach encouraged the imposition of Western aesthetic patterns and designs on *Things Fall Apart* and so prevented the novel from declaring its own unique form. Eurocentrism often resulted in a disregard for the integrity of the novel as a work of art. Judged as if it were attempting to align itself with the Western tradition, *Things Fall Apart* was chastised for lack of plot and character development, weak dramatization, primitive narrative and confused flashbacks. As Charles Larson has shown in *The Emergence of African Fiction*,[7] these misrepresentations resulted from the critics' lack of familiarity with the indigenous literary devices Achebe employed to shape the content of *Things Fall Apart* into a meaningful whole.

More sensitive and responsive to *Things Fall Apart* are those literary critics who have studied the Ibo literary tradition. On the surface, *Things Fall Apart* is deceptively simple. Closer examination reveals a carefully orchestrated interweaving of significant themes—love, compassion, colonialism, honor, individualism and tribal values. The nine essays that follow are written by distinguished scholars and established teachers of African and comparative literature. While the essays vary in scope and depth of treatment of *Things Fall Apart*, together they provide perceptive, at times provocative, interpretations of and insights into *Things Fall Apart*.

For **Angela Smith**, *Things Fall Apart* has a "beautiful simplicity," but its simplicity is deceptive, for beneath the apparent straightforwardness of the narrative is interwoven an intricate network of tantalizing dilemmas. Smith discusses *Things Fall Apart* within the deep tradition of Western literature and Western notions of tragic heroes in order to set forth Achebe's unique accomplishment. Smith provides important insights by tracing Achebe's "flexibility in his use of point of view." Creating a narrative voice whose perspective changes in order to let us see events unfold from various points of view engages the reader and invites us into the novel to participate in the events depicted and draw our own conclusions. Smith makes a compelling argument that "the central unifying and thought-provoking force in the novel is the narrator's voice, which weaves in and out of the characters' consciousness but retains an utterly distinctive quality not present . . . in any other African novel. . . ." While this unique narrative voice may be a "deliberately dislocating experience" for Western readers, it is ideally suited to the purpose of *Things Fall Apart*.

Structural and thematic examination establishes the values Achebe champions in *Things Fall Apart*. Analysis by **Willene P. Taylor** reveals the contrasting values of Umuofia and colonial culture as they are illuminated in Part One and Part Two of the novel. While other critics, including Janmohamed, McDougall, and Opata, exult in the treasures embodied in Part One, Taylor finds Part One "weighted down with ethnological material, which makes the reading plod along rather wearily, unlike the later section of the novel, which moves along rather swiftly to a climax." This first part of the novel is crucial, Taylor does concede, for it demonstrates that the seeds of disintegration lay within the tribal society itself. As the values of the traditional Ibo society are undermined and supplanted by those of Western colonizers, Achebe condemns the British more harshly than he chastens the indigenous people. Taylor concludes that Europeanization has led to a "crisis of the soul," one which "left permanent scars upon the Ibo people and virtually destroyed and perverted their system of values."

Among the important critics who have analyzed the structure of *Things Fall Apart*, **B. Eugene McCarthy** adds the unique perspective afforded by the African oral tradition. McCarthy discusses both individual passages and the structural cadence of Part One of the novel to demonstrate how Achebe creates a rhythmic English prose whose tone is quintessentially African. Similar depth imbues the novel's overall structure as well. McCarthy shows definitively, "The patterning and repetition in Achebe's novel are characteristics of the self-conscious artistry of oral narrative performance, where plot moves by repetition and predictability." The insights McCarthy gains by drawing upon the linguistic heritage of the oral tradition help locate the rhythmic, cultural, thematic and structural centers of the novel, enrich our understanding of the narrative voice, and illustrate another dimension in which the Africanness of the novel resonates: "The style of the novel and its structure thus draw attention to the exquisite tension between traditional

English prose and the unique African and/or Igbo quality Achebe has created. . . ."

The destruction of the traditional Ibo way of life in Umuofia plays out on many levels. One of the most significant, argues **Julian N. Wasserman**, is the linguistic level as the oral tradition of the Ibo becomes fragmented and subsumed by the written tradition of the English. Wasserman discusses language as the "arena in which the cultural struggle between the folkways of the Ibo of Nigeria and the 'High Culture' of their British colonizers is ultimately fought." He carefully delineates the telling differences between the symbolically rich, expansive and redolent language of the Ibos and the more literal-minded reductionism of the literate British. Halfway between the two linguistic worlds stands Okonkwo, himself linguistically deficient as he stammers and resorts to violent action when language fails him. Okonkwo becomes, Wasserman demonstrates, "a symbol for the linguistic breakdown which occurs in the novel." Okonkwo's story, recounted with all of its multiplicities and reverberations by Achebe, becomes reduced to a mere paragraph in the Commissioner's book, a linguistic reductionism "characteristic of all the non-Ibo speaking characters in the novel."

"Can African experience be adequately represented through the alien media (ones that were fashioned to codify an entirely different encounter with reality) of the colonizers' language and literary forms or will these media inevitably alter the nature of African experience in significant ways?" **Abdul Janmohamed** tackles this challenging question in his analysis of the language and structure of *Things Fall Apart* to conclude that Achebe is able to create "a new syncretic form and contribute to the negative dialectics by deterritorializing, to some extent, the English language and the novelistic form." Some of the most compelling points Janmohamed makes arise from his extensive analysis of the linguistic and phenomenological differences between noetic and chirographic cultures. Building on the work of Jack Goody and Walter J. Ong on the nature of oral *versus* chirographic cultures, Janmohamed's discussion offers penetrating analysis of Achebe's use of the English language and the English novel form, transforming each through his artistic syncretism.

According to **Russell McDougall**, crucial insights into *Things Fall Apart* are provided by close examination of the pattern of kinetic action described in the novel. Drawing on the resonant background Robert Farris Thompson sets forth in *African Art in Motion: Icon and Act,* McDougall analyzes Okonkwo's gait: "The iconic significance of Okonkwo's style of walking in defiance of gravity is not only an implicit denial of the power of the earth mother, but also, more generally, an unconscious rejection of the West African way of cultivating divinity 'through richly stabilized traditions of personal balance.'" Okonkwo's gait is an overt manifestation of his denial of his excessive masculinity and repression of his femininity. In a culture which cherishes the balance between earth and sky, feminine and masculine, Okonkwo is "a man aggressive and unbalanced by his defiance of gravity, which represents a denial of the earth." Embodied within Okonkwo's characteristic style of walking is the foreshadowing of his self-destruction in the macabre dance of death.

Damian U. Opata focuses his analysis on Okonkwo's role in the sacrifice of Ikemefuna. Opata demonstrates that Okonkwo's action does not constitute an offense against the Earth. This argument derives its strength from a careful examination of the options available to Okonkwo as an elder of Umuofia. As an elder, Okonkwo had to take a responsible role in carrying out the decree of the Oracle of the Hills and Caves. Further, Opata urges, Okonkwo participates in the sacrifice as a strategy to pretend to Ikemefuna that he was to be returned home. When the other elders fail to do their duty and Ikemefuna runs to Okonkwo for protection, Okonkwo acts instinctively in obedience to the gods' decree: "For Okonkwo, strict adherence to the sacred order takes precedence and allows no human rationalization," Opata writes. Opata does not exonerate Okonkwo but identifies his fault as "uncanny pride in his action," an excess of hubris that occurs not in his striking the fatal blow but in his boasting about his role in the sacrifice. Opata concludes that because Okonkwo is not punished by the traditional ethos for killing Ikemefuna, he then cannot be judged to have committed an offense against the Earth.

Two of my essays are also included here; the first analyzes "Narrative Techniques in *Things Fall Apart*" and the second examines "Okonkwo's Participation in the Killing of His 'Son.'" The study of narrative techniques shows how carefully Achebe modulates the rhythm of the novel, juxtaposing contrasting events. For example, against the joyful harmonic rhythm of the eating of the locusts (*TFA,* pp. 54-55), the withdrawn, controlled formalism of the judgment of the *egwugwu* stands in sharp relief. This pattern of alternation operates throughout the novel to set forth the paradoxes and ironies of Okonkwo's world. The flexibility of Umuofia allows room for Christianity, which in turn contributes to the passing of the traditional ways by fulfilling the needs which the inflexibility of Umuofia left unanswered. This technique of juxtaposition articulates the complexities and contradictions of Umuofia, of Okonkwo, and the dilemma which arises when both confront Christianity.

Paradox also emerges when we analyze Okonkwo as an individual. Examining the series of extreme actions Okonkwo takes to assert his manliness and control reveals that Okonkwo's fatal gift is his predisposition to violence. He commits himself with tragic intensity to becoming the champion of Umuofia's heroic tradition. The very same qualities that establish Okonkwo's greatness also lead to his isolation, his blindness and his ruin. Okonkwo becomes the apotheosis of violent action and as such ultimately destroys himself.

These essays are presented here to guide and enrich the experience of reading *Things Fall Apart*, never to take the place of reading the novel itself. We hope our insights bring the reader back to *Things Fall Apart* to appreciate anew the traditional world of the Ibo people—both what they experienced and what they lost.

Notes

[1] Chinua Achebe, "The Role of the Writer in a New Nation," Ed. G. D. Killam. *African Writers on African Writing.* London: Heinemann, p. 7.

[2] Eustace Palmer, *An Introduction to the African Novel.* London: Heinemann, 1972, p. 48.

[3] R. C. Healy, "Book Review," *New York Herald Tribune* (April 12 1959), 8.

[4] David Hassoldt, "Book Review," *Saturday Review* 42, 18 (January 31, 1959).

[5] Ato Quayson, "Realism, Criticism and the Disguises of Both—A Reading of *Things Fall Apart* with an Evaluation of the Criticism Relating to It," *Research in African Literature* 25 (1994), 3.

[6] Solomon O. Iyasere, "Art, a Simulacrum of Reality—Problems in the Criticism of African Literature," *The Journal of Modern African Studies* II, 3 (1973), 449-450.

[7] Charles Larson, *The Emergence of African Fiction.* Indiana: Indiana University Press, 1972.

The Mouth with Which to Tell of Their Suffering: The Role of Narrator and Reader in Achebe's *Things Fall Apart*

Angela Smith

The complexity of the reader's involvement with the text of *Things Fall Apart* is suggested by the physical appearance of the book, which throws down the gauntlet that Achebe was later to explain more directly in *Morning Yet on Creation Day*:

> Most African writers write out of an African experience and of commitment to an African destiny. For them that destiny does not include a future European identity for which the present is but an apprenticeship. And let no one be fooled by the fact that we may write in English for we intend to do unheard of things with it.[1]

The reader sees from looking at the spine of the book a tension established: the author has a Nigerian name and the title of the novel comes from a poem by a great European poet. The patronizing assumption might be that the novelist wants to establish his credentials as an educated man with his audience, but the novel itself belies this. Something far more subtle is involved: the novelist, in eliciting a response from the reader to the title, and to the title page where the epigraph from "The Second Coming" appears together with the title and the author's name, is creating a link between himself and his reader. If the reader recognizes the quotation from Yeats or knows how to look it up, she is by definition not a part of the Ibo society depicted in the novel, even if she is an Ibo. (Because I am a woman I use "she" where a personal pronoun is required.) She can read English and has access to a world literature so she cannot know what it is to be completely circumscribed in her world view by the village and the tribe. She is to a greater or lesser extent like the District

Commissioner at the end of the novel, a "student of primitive customs" (p. 147), as Achebe himself is in writing the novel. He has said in an interview of the immediate past in Ibo village life that "there's a lot of interesting material there" and he remarks of himself as an observer:

> When I was growing up in my village, it was still possible to catch glimpses of what the complete traditional society must have looked like and one supplemented these impressions with accounts, stories told by old people—like my father. Now, my father, although he was a Christian convert, was very useful to me in this way because he told me how things were in the past.[2]

He was born into a Christian family so that "the sort of civilized life of the village was us."[3] The language he uses to describe how he came to write the novel demonstrates, by its biblical connotations, his links with the world of the District Commissioner: "I now know that my first book, *Things Fall Apart*, was an act of atonement with my past, the ritual return and homage of a prodigal son."[4]

One of the strengths of *Things Fall Apart* is the way in which Achebe sustains the initial impact of the title page through his manipulation of the narrator's voice throughout the novel, and through the sustained self-reflexive irony which is articulated at the end of the book and reveals the connection between Achebe the novelist and the Direct Commissioner:

> As we walked back to the court he thought about that book. Every day brought him some new material. The story of this man who had killed a messenger and hanged himself would make interesting reading. One could almost write a whole chapter on him. Perhaps not a whole chapter but a reasonable paragraph, at any rate.   (pp. 147-148)

The final paragraph of the novel, by commenting through the District Commissioner's consciousness on the business of writing, draws the reader's attention to the writing of the novel itself, as well as to the absurdity of the terms "pacification" and "primitive" in the title of the District Commissioner's book:

> There was so much else to include, and one must be firm in cutting out details. He had already chosen the title of the book, after much thought: *The Pacification of the Primitive Tribes of the Lower Niger*.   (p. 148)

We are by implication invited to compare the subtlety of the
novel we have just read, which devotes more than a chapter to
Okonkwo's story, with the crass book the "civilized" District
Commissioner, with his authentic British "one must be firm,"
plans to write. It is a non-fictional counterpart to one of the
sources of inspiration for Achebe in the conception of *Things
Fall Apart*: Joyce Cary's *Mister Johnson*, "a most superficial picture of—not only of the country, but even of the Nigerian character,"[5] which describes villagers as "bush pagans" and employ-
ment provided by whites as "the world of men":

> It is the bush pagans who have never been outside the
> village before who are most eager to show off their
> feats of acrobatic dancing and to drink the most beer.
> They have already, in five hours, forgotten their dread
> and contempt of the stranger and their resolve to keep
> themselves to themselves. In one afternoon they had
> taken the first essential step out of the world of the
> tribe into the world of men.[6]

The artistry of *Things Fall Apart* lies mainly in conceal-
ment of its art; it appears to be what Angus Wilson called it in
his *Observer* review, "Mr. Achebe's very simple but excellent
novel." Its deceptive simplicity emerges clearly when it is compared with Achebe's other novel about village life, *Arrow of
God*. The structure, plot, language and narrative technique of
Things Fall Apart combine to entertain the reader and lead her
towards an overwhelming question which then proliferates in
her mind into a series of related questions: was Okonkwo right
to kill the messenger as he tried to rouse the lost coherence of
the tribe; were there the seeds of disintegration within the tribe
or were the whites responsible; is the "civilized" tolerance of
men like Obierika destructive; did Okonkwo seal his own fate
when he killed Ikemefuna and if he had not done so could it
have made a difference to the fate of the tribe? The book tanta-
lizes the reader with implicit questions rather like the teasing
question of whether the witches' prophecy leads Macbeth to kill
Duncan thus fulfilling the prophecy. *Arrow of God* tells a similar story but without similar effects, and without the beautiful
simplicity of *Things Fall Apart*.

Uchendu, Okonkwo's uncle and a wise elder in *Things
Fall Apart*, says "there is no story that is not true" (p. 99). There
are stories within stories in *Things Fall Apart*, all with their own
kind of truth which the reader must assess for herself:

> That was the kind of story that Nwoye loved. But he
> now knew that they were for foolish women and chil-
> dren, and he knew that his father wanted him to be a
> man. And so he feigned that he no longer cared for
> women's stories. And when he did this he saw that his
> father was pleased, and no longer rebuked him or beat
> him. So Nwoye and Ikemefuna would listen to
> Okonkwo's stories about tribal wars or how, years ago,
> he had stalked his victim, overpowered him and ob-
> tained his first human head.   (p. 38)

It is not difficult to interpret the moral fables that are part of the
cultural tradition of Okonkwo's people but the question in
Achebe's story of whether "male" stories are superior to "female" ones is harder to resolve, just as it is not easy to encapsu-
late the "truth" of this apparently simple story. In search for the
key, critics have tended to look for defining similarities in Western literature in terms of subject matter rather than the embodiment of a theme. The most common comparisons are with
Hardy's novels and with Greek tragedy.

Certainly in terms of plot there is a faint resemblance between Henchard in *The Mayor of Casterbridge* and Okonkwo, as
David Carroll suggests, but this insignificant link seems to bring
with it a critical vocabulary that has an archaic air about it:

> Of the major divisions of the book, only the trajectory
> of Parts II and III resembles the traditional Western
> well-made novel with conflict-obstacles to be overcome
> by the protagonist. Part I is especially loose, incorpo-
> rating as it does section after section of anthropological
> background.[7]

The idea of the novel consisting of a protagonist overcoming ob-
stacles seems in general to relate much more to nineteenth century than to twentieth century ideas about fiction; it has no bearing on *To the Lighthouse, Ulysses*, or *As I Lay Dying*. This passage is by Charles Larson, who also compares Achebe with Hardy
using the odd phrase "anthropological passages" to describe
Achebe's evocation of the rituals of Okonkwo's tribe:

> Achebe's description in this passage may seem hardly
> relevant to the tragedy he is about to relate. Birds are
> chirruping and although there is the beating of a drum,
> it is not, so far as can be determined, in any sense in-
> tended as foreboding. Rather, it is the drum and music
> for 'dancing and a great feast.' Even the sun breaking
> through the leaves and branches evokes no mood of im-
> minent tragedy or despair, but, if anything, one of

> peacefulness and serenity. If one compares this passage
> with that in Joseph Conrad's *Heart of Darkness* when
> Marlow is going up the river in search of Kurtz, it is
> easy to see how little Achebe uses description in a
> Western sense to evoke mood and atmosphere. Rather,
> it is that his description, when it is present, is used
> more directly for functional than for aesthetic pur-
> poses.[8]

The stereotype behind this passage is clearly a nineteenth century Western notion of tragedy in fiction; drums are ominous in
Western culture but are used for a variant of purposes in Africa.
The power of the passage in the novel that Larson is referring to
derives from the fact that the point of view shifts delicately between the omniscient narrator and Ikemefuna, the innocent
child who trusts Okonkwo and so goes to his death cheerfully
observant and unaware of the purpose of the expedition. The
reader knows what he does not know, unlike the reader of *Heart
of Darkness*, so that ominous drums would be like tense music
in Hollywood B movies:

> The footway had now become a narrow line in the heart
> of the forest. The short trees and sparse undergrowth
> which surrounded the men's village began to give way
> to giant trees and climbers which perhaps had stood
> from the beginning of things, untouched by the axe and
> the bush-fire. The sun breaking through their leaves
> and branches threw a pattern of light and shade on the
> sandy footway.
>   Ikemefuna heard a whisper close behind him and
> turned around sharply.   (pp. 41-42)

This serves an aesthetic purpose but is economical and spare,
nothing like Hardy's use of landscape. It is not ominous, nor
does it need to be as the reader knows all too well what is about
to happen. It has the simple poignancy which the natural world
possesses for those who are about to leave it, though this is the
reader's perception, not Ikemefuna's. Achebe uses natural description in his characteristically unobtrusive way, but it provides a sensuous image, not ethnological background:

> There were no stars in the sky because there was a rain-
> cloud. Fireflies went about with their tiny green
> lamps, which only made the darkness more profound.
> Between Chielo's outbursts the night was alive with
> the shrill tremor of forest insects woven into the dark-
> ness.   (p. 73)

Things Fall Apart is radically different from Hardy's fiction as an experience for the reader because it is taut and ascetic, with no intervention from the narrator of this kind, from *Jude the Obscure*:

> Somebody might have come along that way who would have asked him his trouble, and might have cheered him by saying that his notions were further advanced than those of his grammarian. But nobody did come, because nobody does; and under the crushing recognition of his gigantic error Jude continued to wish himself out of the world.[9]

Similarly, an attempt to define *Things Fall Apart* by comparison with Greek or Shakespearean tragedy causes confusion rather than clarification. It suggests a fatalistic helplessness about Okonkwo which cannot be reconciled with the reader's experience of Okonkwo as a character:

> For tragedy implies the working out in men's lives of a rigorous fatality that transcends the individual's ability to comprehend or to arrest its pre-ordained course of events. . . . His accidental killing of a villager and his subsequent exile from Umuofia are the workings of a blind fate crossing his path to his own conception of self-realisation. . . . For Okonkwo's inflexibility, his tragic flaw, is a reflection of his society.[10]

Achebe makes it clear in the novel that Okonkwo is not a tragic hero by the relationship he creates between Okonkwo and the reader. Okonkwo is from the beginning a figure who is both impressive and comic, but he never commands the intellectual respect that Nwoye and Obierika do. Okonkwo's insights are mistaken, though the reader must realize this for herself. Again the point of view shifts and the omniscient narrator recedes without comment, inviting the reader to be amused and exasperated by Okonkwo's sexist limitations:

> He, Okonkwo, was called a flaming fire. How could he have begotten a woman for a son? At Nwoye's age Okonkwo had already become famous throughout Umuofia for his wrestling and his fearlessness.
>
> He sighed heavily, and as if in sympathy the smouldering log also sighed. And immediately Okonkwo's eyes were opened and he saw the whole matter clearly. Living fire begets cold, impotent ash. He sighed again, deeply.   (pp. 108-109)

He does not reveal one crucial tragic flaw; he is not simply in-flexible but incapable, through pride and fear, of learning as he shows here. It does not seem to occur to him that he is in any way responsible for what happens to Nwoye. The reader recog-nizes despondently that Okonkwo has leant nothing from his exile when he returns from his motherland and mourns "for the clan, which he saw breaking up and falling apart, and he mourned for the warlike men of Umuofia, who had so unac-countably become soft like women" (p. 129).

This is confirmed when he lies in bed before the final vil-lage meeting, determined to plan his own revenge if the tribe succumbs to "womanish wisdom" (p. 141). Okonkwo never rec-ognizes his own limitations and dies without self-knowledge, a victim of his own inability to mediate or change as Obierika does. "Rigorous fatality" and "blind fate" seem to have little to do with his death; a much more tangible cause is suggested. Both Okonkwo and the colonial powers are uncompromising. Okonkwo recognizes that his people are not as adamant as he when he hears them asking "Why did he do it?" after he has killed the messenger. The one incident in the novel that can be attributed to "fate" is the death of Ezeudu's son, but as I shall show, Achebe suggests that Okonkwo is morally responsible for his death, and certainly he should not have been brandishing his loaded gun when he is notorious for his lack of control over it. It could almost be said to symbolize Okonkwo's aggressive but undisciplined masculinity.

Achebe told Lewis Nkosi in an interview, "I used to like Hemingway; and I used to like Conrad, I used to like Conrad par-ticularly."[11] Without wishing to substitute one unhelpful com-parison for another, one can see the relevance of this remark to Achebe's own fiction. He requires a participating reader who perceives the questions and is sensitive to the way in which the language of the novel controls his responses. The tone of the depiction of Unoka and Okonkwo is subtle and ironic, creating uncertainty in the reader. The opening of the novel indicates that Okonkwo is admired by his society: "His fame rested on solid personal achievements." But although he is "as slippery as a fish in water," the tone of the third paragraph modulates and the reader begins to find the picture of Okonkwo's oppressive snores, and his habit of pummeling people instead of speaking to them, comic and reductive:

> He breathed heavily, and it as said that, when he
> slept, his wives and children in their out-houses could
> hear him breathe. When he walked, his heels hardly
> touched the ground and he seemed to walk on springs, as
> if he was going to pounce on somebody. And he did
> pounce on people quite often. He had a slight stammer
> and whenever he was angry and could not get his words
> out quickly enough, he would use his fists. He had no
> patience with unsuccessful men. He had no patience
> with his father.

The grammar and brevity of the last two sentences seem to
mimic Okonkwo's impatience.

Unoka is introduced as a failure but the flowing sentence
structure used of him compared with the terse machine-gun fire
opening paragraph makes him appealing to the reader, as does
his sensuous response to the natural world, and the use of
phrases for him that are rich in positive connotations: "beaming
with blessedness and peace," "dazzling beauty," "loved . . . loved
. . . loved . . . loved":

> Unoka would play with them, his face beaming with
> blessedness and peace . . . Unoka loved the good fare
> and the good fellowship, and he loved this season of
> the year, when the rains had stopped and the sun rose
> every morning with dazzling beauty . . . Unoka loved it
> all, and he loved the first kites that returned with the
> dry season, and the children who sang songs of welcome
> to them. He would remember his own childhood, how
> he had often wandered around looking for a kite sailing
> leisurely against the blue sky. As soon as he found one
> he would sing with his whole being, welcoming it back
> from its long journey, and asking it if it had brought
> home any lengths of cloth.   (p. 5)

It is impossible to imagine the bouncing Okonkwo wandering
and gazing at the sky, yet in singing his song Unoka is maintaining a village tradition. Unoka is an artist who hates war; again
the juxtaposition of flowing sentences evoking Unoka's pleasure
in music followed by the abrupt no-nonsense grammar used for
Okoye belies the statement that Unoka is a failure, and implicitly
questions the criteria used to determine who is a success and
who isn't:

> He could hear in his mind's ear the blood-stirring and
> intricate rhythms of the *ekwe* and the *udu* and the
> *ogene*, and he could hear his own flute weaving in and
> out of them, decorating them with a colourful and
> plaintive tune. The total effect was gay and brisk but if

> one picked out the flute as it went up and down and then
> broke up into short snatches, one saw that there was
> sorrow and grief there.
>   Okoye was also a musician.   He played on the
> *ogene*. But he was not a failure like Unoka. He had a
> large barn full of yams and he had three wives.   And
> now he was going to take the Idemili title.   (p. 5)

The reader surely laughs with Unoka, and at Okoye, in Unoka's
incredulous and delighted mirth over being asked to repay a
debt, and in his witty use of the proverb of the sun shining on
those who stand:

> 'Look at those lines of chalk. . . . Each group there rep-
> resents a debt to someone, and each stroke is one hun-
> dred cowries. You see, I owe that man a thousand
> cowries. But he has not come to wake me up in the
> morning for it. I shall pay you, but not today. Our el-
> ders say that the sun will shine on those who stand be-
> fore it shines on those who kneel under them. I shall
> pay my big debts first.' And he took another pinch of
> snuff, as if that was paying the big debts first.   (p. 6)

If the reader is attentive she will observe a quality in Unoka
which Okonkwo lacks, and which is admired in Ibo society:
"among the Ibo the art of conversation is regarded very highly"
(p. 5). The art of conversation is shown to be dependent on wit
and sensitivity to human need; Ikemefuna, like Unoka and
some of the women in the novel, possesses it, but stuttering and
impatient Okonkwo does not.

Okonkwo is defined for the reader through the comparison with his father in the first three chapters, and the apparent
approval of Okonkwo is constantly undercut by the language,
and "masculine" grammar:

> He was a man of action, a man of war. Unlike his
> father he could stand the look of blood. In Umuofia's
> latest war he was the first to bring home a human
> head. That was his fifth head; and he was not an old
> man yet. On great occasions such as the funeral of a vil-
> lage celebrity he drank his palm-wine from his first
> human head.   (pp. 7-8)

Okonkwo hates gentleness as well as idleness because his father
loves both, and again the terse sentence structure reveals this as
a crippling limitation in Okonkwo's human awareness:

> His father, Unoka, who was then an ailing man, had
> said to him during that terrible harvest month: 'Do not
> despair. I know you will not despair. You have a

> manly and a proud heart. A proud heart can survive a
> general failure because such a failure does not prick its
> pride. It is more difficult and more bitter when a man
> fails *alone*.'
>   Unoka was like that in his last days. His love of
> talk had grown with age and sickness. It tried
> Okonkwo's patience beyond words.   (p. 18)

Okonkwo is in fact almost always literally beyond words; he can
only articulate rage, aggression and contempt, which limits both
his understanding and experience and makes him impervious
to Unoka's gentle loving wisdom. His inarticulacy causes
Nwoye's alienation from the tribe and prevents Okonkwo's en-
joyment of feasts, where the main pleasure lies in conversation:
"He was always uncomfortable sitting around for days waiting
for a feast or getting over it" (p. 27). His lack of gentleness towards his sons contains the seeds of his own destruction; his
harshness to them contrasts painfully with Unoka's gentle
words to him about the yam harvest:

> Sometimes Okonkwo gave them a few yams each to
> prepare. But he always found fault with their effort,
> and he said so with much threatening. . . . Inwardly
> Okonkwo knew that the boys were still too young to un-
> derstand fully the difficult art of preparing seed-yams.
> But he thought that one could not begin too early. Yam
> stood for manliness.   (p. 23)

The final painful irony of the comparison between
Okonkwo and his father is that, though they are totally dissimi-
lar and Okonkwo despises his father, their ultimate fate is the
same. Unoka "died of the swelling which was an abomination
to the earth goddess" (p. 13) and so he had no burial but was left
to die in the Evil Forest, pathetically tootling on his flute.
Though the manner of Okonkwo's death is quite different, a vil-
lager tells the District Commissioner, "'It is an abomination for a
man to take his own life. It is an offence against the Earth'" (p.
147). Again the reader is left to speculate about the link: have
both characters a bad *chi* or personal god, which means they are
fated to meet a disastrous end, or are they morally responsible
for what happens to them? Both are inflexible, Okonkwo in
conforming too rigorously to tribal conceptions of manliness
and Unoka in refusing to conform at all.

The Achebe's method in the early chapters creates uncertainty
in the reader though the narrator never overtly questions the
values of the tribe. The first part of the novel is more than "the

piling up of ethnological material." It demands active participation from the reader. The image of the unfortunate, lazy and
appealing Unoka being carried off to the Evil Forest to die and
taking his flute with him sticks in the reader's mind and forms
one of the unobtrusive links which are a recurrent and persua-
sive device in the novel. Nwoye, Okonkwo's son, is sensitive
and thoughtful, qualities which Okonkwo defines as "incipient
laziness" (p. 10). When he meets Ikemefuna he is immediately
drawn to him because "he could fashion out flutes from bamboo
stems and even from the elephant grass" (p. 20). This suggests
that Ikemefuna may resemble Unoka, as he proves to do in positive but not negative respects, but there is also something
vaguely ominous about it, reminding us of Unoka's cruel death
and the phrase "the ill-fated lad" (p. 6) used of Ikemefuna at the
end of the first chapter.

These apparently random connections occur particularly
in relation to Ikemefuna. When he is being taken to his death
the music of an *ozo* dance, for a man assuming a new title, is
carried to the assassination party on the wind from a distant
clan, and the reader is reminded of Okonkwo's remorseless ambition to reach the highest title, which drives him to conceal
what he considers to be weakness and to assist in the murder of a
boy who is virtually his own son. This brief passage is full of
similar associations. Ikemefuna sings in his head to comfort
himself on what the reader knows to be a sinister journey, just
as Unoka played his flute for the same reason. When Ikemefuna is eventually struck down, Achebe includes a little detail
about the pot he carries: "The pot fell and broke in the sand" (p.
43). This intensifies the restrained pathos of the scene as it reminds us of Ikemefuna's sensitivity in an early scene, of domestic contentment. Obiageli, Nwoye's little sister, comes home in
tears because she has broken her water pot by playing with it:

> Nwoye's younger brothers were about to tell their
> mother the true story of the accident when Ikemefuna
> looked at them sternly and they held their peace.
>
> (p. 31)

He is clearly one of the family.

The unstated morality of the novel establishes itself in the
reader's mind through similar unemphasized links, all connecting with Okonkwo's involvement in the murder of Ikemefuna
and with the stress on kinship and particularly the relationship
between father and son. Okonkwo takes part in the murder of

Ikemefuna although Ezeudu, the oldest man in the village, tells him not to:

> 'That boy calls you father. Do not bear a hand in his death.' Okonkwo was surprised, and was about to say something when the old man continued:
> 'Yes, Umuofia has decided to kill him. The Oracle of the Hills and Caves has pronounced it. They will take him outside Umuofia as is the custom, and kill him there. But I want you to have nothing to do with it.'   (p. 40)

Obierika's comment is even more ominous:

> 'You know very well, Okonkwo, that I am not afraid of blood; and if anyone tells you that I am, he is telling a lie. And let me tell you one thing, my friend. If I were you I would have stayed at home. What you have done will not please the Earth. It is the kind of action for which the goddess wipes out whole families.'   (p. 46)

When the reader encounters the description of the second boy killed, this time accidentally, by Okonkwo she is simply invited to make connections for herself:

> In the centre of the crowd a boy lay in a pool of blood. It was the dead man's sixteen-year old son, who with his brothers and half-brothers had been dancing the traditional farewell to their father. Okonkwo's gun had exploded and a piece of iron had pieced the boy's heart.
>   (p. 86)

The implication is that Obierika's prophecy is coming true. Okonkwo has already disrupted a festival twice, once in the farcical scene when he shot his second wife, and once, more seriously, when it was thought that he had offended the Earth Goddess by beating his youngest wife during the Week of Peace. The eccentric gun links the two scenes. Ezeudu's son is a kinsman of Okonkwo, and the accidental murder means that Okonkwo has committed another crime against the Earth Goddess but also that she may by having her revenge on Okonkwo for his part in killing his "son," Ikemefuna.

The pattern of father/son relationships suggests that Okonkwo's limitations cripple him most as a son and as a father. Though he condemns the Christian dictum "Blessed is he who forsakes his father and his mother for my sake" he himself sets the pattern of filial contempt, for even as a little boy he "resented his father's failure and weakness" (p. 10). What Nwoye takes to be Okonkwo's betrayal of Ikemefuna alters him just as he is be-

ginning to turn into the aggressively masculine son that
Okonkwo longs for. The narrative shifts to Nwoye's point of
view and reveals that he holds his father personally responsible
for Ikemefuna's death:

> As soon as his father walked in, that night, Nwoye
> knew that Ikemefuna had been killed, and something
> seemed to give way inside him, like the snapping of a
> tightened bow. . . . It was after such a day at the farm
> during the last harvest that Nwoye had felt for the
> first time a snapping inside him like the one he now
> felt. They were returning home with baskets of yams
> from a distant farm across the stream when they had
> heard the voice of an infant crying in the thick forest.
> A sudden hush had fallen on the women, who had been
> talking, and they had quickened their steps. Nwoye
> had heard that twins were put in earthenware pots and
> thrown away in the forest, but he had never yet come
> across them. A vague chill had descended on him and
> his head had seemed to swell, like a solitary walker
> at night who passes an evil spirit on the way. Then
> something had given way inside him. It descended on
> him again, this feeling, when his father walked in,
> that night after killing Ikemefuna.   (p. 43)

The snapping bow image implies an instinctive rejection of aggressive masculinity. The fact that Nwoye takes the Christian
name Isaac suggests that he sees himself as the victim of his father's deeply held beliefs. In the chapter preceding Nwoye's
conversion Okonkwo, in exile, asks how he can thank Obierika
for his kindness:

> 'I can tell you,' said Obierika. 'Kill one of your sons for me.
> 'That will not be enough,' said Okonkwo.
> 'Then kill yourself,' said Obierika.   (p. 100)

This reflects that past and anticipates the future. By killing the
boy, Ikemefuna, who was virtually his son, Okonkwo had alienated his real son to such an extent that Nwoye says '"He is not
my father"' (p. 101) and Okonkwo tells his other sons that
Nwoye '"is no longer my son or your brother"' (p. 121). He has
also made his own death inevitable because he feels intense personal bitterness against all white men for what they have done
to his family. He fails to recognize his own partial responsibility
for what has happened:

> How else could he express his great misfortune and ex-
> ile and now his despicable son's behaviour? Now that
> he had time to think of it, his son's crime stood out in

> its stark enormity. To abandon the gods of one's father
> and go about with a lot of effeminate men clucking like
> old hens was the very depth of abomination. Suppose
> when he died all his male children decided to follow
> Nwoye's steps and abandon their ancestors? Okonkwo
> felt a cold shudder run through him at the terrible
> prospect, like the prospect of annihilation. He saw
> himself and his father crowding round their ancestral
> shrine waiting in vain for worship and sacrifice and
> finding nothing but ashes of bygone days, and his chil-
> dren all the while praying to the white man's god. If
> such a thing were ever to happen, he, Okonkwo, would
> wipe them off the face of the earth.   (p. 108)

His remedy is, as usual, a violent one, in spite of the fact that he
has by now killed two promising boys. There is an implicit sug-
gestion that, like Nwoye, Okonkwo has forsaken his mother,
both in scorn for "feminine" qualities and in what Uchendu says
to Obierika and Okonkwo:

> 'Those were good days when a man had friends in dis-
> tant lands. Your generation does not know that. You
> stay at home, afraid of your next-door neighbour. Even
> a man's motherland is strange to him nowadays.' He
> looked at Okonkwo.   (p. 96)

Achebe manipulates the reader subtly through his unobtrusive
but suggestive linking technique.

Achebe encourages the reader to perceive unstated connections by his own flexibility in his use of point of view.
Larson states:

> Whereas the other twenty-four chapters are told
> strictly from the point of view of the objective African
> novelist, the twenty-fifth chapter shifts the view-
> point back and forth between Obierika and the white
> District Commissioner, for much of the action in this
> chapter is seen through the eyes of the latter.[12]

This is factually inaccurate as the narrator does not use
Obierika's point of view, though he gives his opinion; the impact of the final chapter for the reader who has been absorbed in
Umuofia is that it is seen entirely through the unsympathetic
eyes of the District Commissioner, and the delicate Ibo art of
conversation which has been revealed through the novel is reduced to this:

> One of the most infuriating habits of these people was
> their love of superfluous words, he thought.   (p. 146)

Yet he thinks of himself as civilized: "In the many years in which he had toiled to bring civilization to different parts of Africa he had learnt a number of things" (p. 147).

The most moving use of shifting point of view occurs when Ikemefuna is walking to his death thinking about Okonkwo with the reader aware that Okonkwo plans to kill him; Ikemefuna's childish vulnerability is revealed:

> Although he had felt uneasy at first, he was not afraid now. Okonkwo walked behind him. He could hardly imagine that Okonkwo was not his real father.   He had never been fond of his real father and at the end of three years he had become very distant indeed. But his mother and his three-year-old sister . . . of course she would not be three now, but six. Would he recognize her now? She must have grown quite big. How his mother would weep for joy, and thank Okonkwo for having looked after him so well and for bringing him back.
>
> (p. 42)

By moving into Okonkwo's consciousness frequently the reader is invited, without comment from the narrator, to draw her own conclusions.   There is a sudden shift of point of view at the moment of the murder:

> Why had Okonkwo withdrawn to the rear? Ikemefuna felt his legs melting under him. And he was afraid to look back.
>
> As the man who had cleared his throat drew up and raised his matchet, Okonkwo looked away. He heard the blow. The pot fell and broke in the sand. He heard Ikemefuna cry, 'My father, they have killed me!' as he ran towards him. Dazed with fear Okonkwo drew his matchet and cut him down. He was afraid of being thought weak.   (p. 43)

The chapter in which Okonkwo returns to Umuofia ends with this paragraph:

> Okonkwo was deeply grieved. And it was not just a personal grief. He mourned for the clan, which he saw breaking up and falling apart, and he mourned for the warlike men of Umuofia, who had so unaccountably become soft like women.   (p. 129)

This reveals that he has learned nothing from his stay in his motherland of the "feminine" qualities that Unoka, Nwoye and Ikemefuna possess and that Uchendu praises:

> 'When a father beats a child, it seeks sympathy in its mother's hut. A man belongs to his fatherland when

> things are good and life is sweet. But when there is sor-
> row and bitterness he finds refuge in his motherland.
> Your mother is there to protect you. She is buried there.
> And that is why we say that mother is supreme.'
>
> (p. 94)

The central unifying and thought-provoking force in the
novel is the narrator's voice, which weaves in and out of the
characters' consciousness but retains an utterly distinctive quality not present in *Arrow of God* or in any other African novel
depicting the clash of cultures in a rural setting. David Carroll
writes:

> The novel is narrated in the third person, but there is no
> suggestion of an omniscient narrator scrutinising and
> analysing the customs and habits of this Igbo commu-
> nity. The voice is that of a wise and sympathetic elder
> of the tribe who has witnessed time and time again the
> cycle of the seasons and the accompanying rituals in the
> villages.[13]

Lynn Innes agrees that "the narrative voice is primarily a recre-
ation of the persona which is heard in the tales, history, proverbs
and poetry belonging to an oral tradition."[14] This is partly true
but it is irreconcilable with a passage like this:

> The night was very quiet. It was always quiet except on
> moonlight nights. Darkness held a vague terror for
> these people, even the bravest among them. Children
> were warned not to whistle at night for fear of evil
> spirits. Dangerous animals became even more sinister
> and uncanny in the dark. A snake was never called by
> its name at night, because it would hear. It was called
> a string.   (p. 7)

There is surely a deliberate, recurrent and disconcerting shift in
the narrator's voice between the timeless tones of the story-teller
in the oral tradition using proverbs, myths and local words, and
the cold detachment of the anthropological observer, discernible
in the phrase "for these people," which recurs. We are reminded of it when the District Commissioner thinks irritably
about "these people's" infuriating habits. Another link is forged;
the narrator clearly understands the society he is depicting but he
speaks the same language as the District Commissioner, so he
cannot entirely belong to Umuofia.

The famous "palm-oil" metaphor can seem disparaging
and ironic since it follows another distancing anthropological
observation:

> Having spoken plainly so far, Okoye said the next half
> a dozen sentences in proverbs. Among the Ibo the art of
> conversation is regarded very highly, and proverbs are
> the palm-oil with which words are eaten.   (p. 5)

It is difficult to judge the tone of this; similar examples abound. In the one that follows, the role of the rain-maker seems to be mocked by the sophisticated vocabulary of the narrator, particularly in the use of the word "dynamism":

> He could not stop the rain now, just as he would not at-
> tempt to start it in the heart of the dry season, without
> serious danger to his own health.   The personal dy-
> namism required to counter the forces of these extremes
> of weather would be far too great for the human frame.
>   (p. 24)

There are pervasive reminders throughout even the first part of the novel that the world described is irretrievable, and that the reader cannot assume comfortably that she is listening to a timeless tale, for the title, epigraph, and quotations like "nature . . . red in the tooth and claw" (p. 9) make her aware that the narrator is deceiving her when he assumes the voice of the Ibo teller of tales. The point of the novel is that "the very soul of the tribe wept for a great evil that was coming—its own death" (p. 132). It would be meaningless for Achebe to recreate the teller's voice with total confidence as that is part of what was destroyed by the colonial powers. If he can recreate it fully, it is not lost, but his occasionally jarring tone reminds the reader that the narrator knows what the teller of tales was like but he cannot be one because of what happened to the Ibo people in the late nineteenth century.

The narrator's almost schizophrenic voice is not a matter of authorial carelessness but is a conscious device to make manifest the meaning of the title. The narrator has two modes of expression, and two sets of vocabulary which he deliberately juxtaposes against one another. In the following passage the "live coals" image is drawn from village experience but "coiffure" comes from a different area of experience altogether:

> For two or three moons the sun had been gathering
> strength till it seemed to breathe a breath of fire on the
> earth. All the grass had long been scorched brown, and
> the sand felt like live coals to the feet. Evergreen trees
> wore a dusty coat of brown. . . . Palm trees swayed as
> the wind combed their leaves into flying crests like
> strange and fantastic coiffure.   (pp. 91-92)

It is rather like Achebe's treatment of time in the novel, which confirms the duality of the narrator's voice. He deliberately plunges the reader into time measured by seasons, and events within living memory; beyond that, time cannot be measured:

> Its most potent war-medicine was as old as the clan it-
> self. Nobody knew how old.   (p. 8)

> He recovered from his illness only a few days before
> the Week of Peace began. And that was also the year
> Okonkwo broke the peace, and was punished, as was
> the custom, by Ezeani, the priest of the earth goddess.
>   (p. 21)

> Giant trees and climbers which perhaps had stood from
> the beginning of things, untouched by the axe and the
> bush fire.   (p. 41)

Abruptly the reader is jerked from this unrecorded time, where history quickly becomes myth, into recent historical time, with the arrival of the missionaries and the messenger's announce-ment: "'They have a queen'" (p. 127). Achebe enables the reader to enact, to a limited extent, the shock the characters experience with the arrival of the white man. For Western readers it is a deliberately dislocating experience, revealing that in Achebe, his people and other rural African communities have "'found the mouth with which to tell of their suffering'" (p. 125).

Notes

Page references are taken from: Chinua Achebe, *Things Fall Apart*, London: Heinemann, 1976 edition.

[1] Chinua Achebe, *Morning Yet on Creation Day*, London: Heinemann, 1975, p. 7.
[2] Dennis Duerden and Cosmo Pieterse, eds., *African Writers Talking*, London: Heinemann, 1972, p. 9.
[3] Ibid., p. 5.
[4] *Morning Yet on Creation Day*, p. 70.
[5] *African Writers Talking*, p. 4.
[6] Joyce Cary, *Mister Johnson*, London: Michael Joseph, 1952, p. 160.
[7] Charles Larson, *The Emergence of African Fiction*, London: Macmillan, 1978, p. 62.
[8] Ibid., p. 45.
[9] Thomas Hardy, *Jude the Obscure*, London: Macmillan, 1906, chapter 4.

[10] C. L. Innes and Bernth Lindfors, eds., *Critical Perspectives on Chinua Achebe*, London: Heinemann, 1979, Irele, pp. 10-14.

[11] *African Writers Talking*, p. 6.

[12] *The Emergence of African Fiction*, pp. 57-58.

[13] David Carroll, *Chinua Achebe*, London: Macmillan, 1980, p. 31.

[14] *Critical Perspectives*, p. 111.

The Search for Values Theme in Chinua Achebe's Novel, *Things Fall Apart*: A Crisis of the Soul

Willene P. Taylor

One of the main themes in Chinua Achebe's novel, *Things Fall Apart*, is the search for values in a world that is constantly beset by change. Having taken his title from William Butler Yeats' poem, "The Second Coming," Achebe, like Yeats, presents in vivid terms his interpretation of the cyclical view of history. In Yeats' work, the vision of human history projects a succession of "gyres" or epochal cycles. The first of these cycles, the pre-Christian era, gives way to the age ushered in by the nativity of Christ, which in turn will be followed by another and more terrifyingly unknown cycle—the new Bethlehem of another era or "coming." Achebe's novel, *Things Fall Apart*, like Yeats' poem, also presents the vision of human history in a series of epochal cycles but from an African rather than a European perspective. The first of Achebe's cycles, Ibo tribal life before the coming of the British to Nigeria near the end of the nineteenth century makes way for the beginning of twentieth century Europeanization of Africa with all its implied consequences for still another era—the future of post-colonial Africa.

In using Yeats' European material to draw a contrast between the various periods of Ibo history, Achebe is able to accomplish two things. First of all, through manipulating the Yeatsian theme about the changes inevitable in human history, the novelist succeeds in showing that the sense of historical decay, continuity, and rebirth is not only characteristic of the European tradition but also of the African tradition. Second, by exploiting this European literature and historiography, ironically Achebe is able to reverse the white man's narrow definition of culture and history.

On one level of *Things Fall Apart*, the novelist depicts the plight of the protagonist Okonkwo, the character most opposed to change, in trying to hold on to the traditional values of his society amidst the imposition of a powerful, alien force that seeks to undermine these values and practices. On still another level, and perhaps more importantly, the novelist depicts the predicament of the entire clan in preserving these values when they become threatened by another and more puissant way of life.

Things Fall Apart is the first of Achebe's four novels.[1] Consisting of twenty-four books, the work vividly recreates African tribal life in the 1890's when the British colonialists first came to Africa and imposed their way of life upon the indigenous people. As is readily apparent from even a cursory reading of the novel, Europe's contact with Africa ultimately led to a dissolution of the values that some Ibos held sacred, and hence to a falling apart of the clan.

In analyzing the coming of the white man to Nigeria and the resulting disintegration of traditional African society, Achebe uses the vehicle of the novel as an act of self-definition. Prior to the writing and publication of *Things Fall Apart*, Achebe had become increasingly disturbed by the portraits of the African as the noble savage depicted in the works of European writers. To a person, these European men of letters generally tended to reinforce the belief that colonialism was an agent of enlightenment to so-called "primitive" peoples without a valid value system or civilization of their own. Hence, Africa was pictured as the "dark" continent, inhabited by childlike, superstitious, and fearful people only too ready to welcome, and, indeed worship the white man. Both Joseph Conrad's *The Heart of Darkness* and Joyce Cary's *Mister Johnson*, for example—works that Achebe had read and digested—painted just such a demeaning picture of the African people.

Achebe grew up at a time when Africans were beginning to oppose European rule through political action and were also beginning to question with increasing vigor and clarity the cultural assumptions used to justify that rule. Hence, the novelist began to question and to object to the demeaning portrait of the African depicted in the novels of Conrad and Cary. As Achebe, for example, points out in one of his interviews, the writer's first duty is to demonstrate

that African people did not hear of culture for the first
time from Europeans: that societies were not mindless
but frequently had a philosophy of great depth and
beauty, that they had poetry and above all, they had
dignity.[2]

Structurally, *Things Fall Apart* is divided into two main
sections.[3] The first section, consisting of chapters 1-14, gives a
description of the traditional mores or values of Ibo society prac-
ticed by Okonkwo and the members of his clan before Africa's
tragic encounter with Europe; and the second section, compris-
ing chapters 15-24, chronicles the "falling apart" and annihilation of Okonkwo, his family, his clan, and his value system after
Africa's introduction and exposure to European influences.

Section one of novel is highly anthropological but sets the
stage for the conflict in values in the last half of the work. As
Charles Larson has suggested, this tension is introduced early in
the novel "because the old African way of life typified by
Okonkwo, is unable to adapt to the new, to the West."[4] Here, in
this first section of the novel where a description of traditional
life in the Ibo hinterland is established, there is virtually no plot
as such, especially in the sense of a well-developed narrative or a
major conflict involving the protagonist, Okonkwo. Rather, the
narrative is weighted down with ethnological material, which
makes the reading plod along rather wearily, unlike the latter
section of the novel which moves rather swiftly to a climax.
This weightiness of the narrative in the first part of the work is
due not so much to Achebe's lack of narrative skill, but to his
successful attempt to carry out his initial purpose; that is, to
show that the traditional life and value system of this rather rigorously ordered and secure African society will fall apart when it
becomes exposed to western influences, represented by Christianity and the British colonial rule. Also, the lack of a readily
apparent plot in Part I allows Achebe to give a detailed catalogue
of Ibo values and customs and relate them not only to Okonkwo,
the main character, but also simultaneously to members of
Okonkwo's Umuofian clan.

When the novel begins, the reader is immediately told of
the values revered and respected by the Ibo people. For example,
"Age was respected among his people," the narrator states, "but
achievement was revered."[5] It is just this emphasis on
achievement that leads Okonkwo, the protagonist of the book, to
become obsessed with the weakness in his father Unoka—an ob-

session so strong that it becomes the ruling force of his entire being. Even as a little boy, the narrator commented, Okonkwo

> . . . had resented his father's failure and weakness, and
> even now he still remembered how he had suffered
> when a playmate had told him that his father was
> *agbala*. That was how Okonkwo first came to know
> that *agbala* was not only another name for a woman, it
> could also mean a man who had taken no title. And so
> Okonkwo was ruled by one passion—to hate everything
> that his father Unoka had loved. One of those things
> was gentleness and another was idleness.[6]

Okonkwo becomes so obsessed with his father's weakness
and with demonstrating his own perceived superior masculinity
that, indeed, the reader is not surprised when this masculinity
later turns out to take the forms of child-abuse and wife-beating,
the latter having happened during the Week of Peace. And although beating one's wife during the Week of Peace can bring
destruction to this intradependent and tightly knit clan, it makes
little difference to Okonkwo who is excessive sometimes to the
point of obnoxiousness in his adherence to the traditional values of his society, and who thinks that regardless of the significance of the Week of Peace, a man ought not stop beating his
wife halfway through the act. By assigning the traits of excess
and uncompromise to the protagonist of the novel, Achebe implies that Okonkwo's inflexible adherence to what he perceives
to be the values of his society without any real analysis, questioning brings about his own destruction in the end and, by extension, the destruction or falling apart of the entire clan. For, in
spite of Okonkwo's heroic and noble stature in the novel,[7] he is
seen in some instances as less sensible than the characters who
can adjust to change with time and circumstances.

For, to be sure, although Achebe has said that Africa had a
well-developed and dignified culture long before the Europeans
imposed upon it an alien way of life, he has also stated that

> We cannot pretend that our past was one long techni-
> color idyll. We have to admit that like other people's
> past ours had its good and bad sides.[8]

Hence, it seems clear that in looking back toward the dissolution
of Ibo society and its values in *Things Fall Apart*, Achebe
demonstrates through excessive actions and uncompromising
stances of Okonkwo that the disintegration of the Umuofian

clan was merely hastened, not entirely caused by European intervention.

Ironically, it is Okonkwo's obsession with the adherence
to the Ibo value system which causes him to lose his son,
Nwoye, to the European way of life. Two incidents are responsible for Nwoye's breaking the bond with his father and his reassessment and rejection of some of the mores of his society:
Okonkwo's killing of his adopted son, Ikemefuna, and the tribal
practice of leaving twins to die in the Evil Forest. The first
caused by a flaw in Okonkwo's personal character and the second
caused by the customs of society both result in Nwoye's running
to the white man's religion and church for relief, an act which
tears away at the very fabric of Okonkwo's soul.

In participating in the killing of his adopted son, Ikemefuna, Okonkwo proves what the omniscient narrator says about
him, that he "was a man not of thought but of action."[9] Unlike
his friend, Obierika, who thinks through his actions, Okonkwo
does just the opposite and tries to rationalize the killing by citing
a proverb and then perverting its meaning:

> 'The Earth cannot punish me for obeying her messenger,'
> Okonkwo said. 'A child's fingers are not scalded by a
> piece of yam which its mother puts into its palm.'[10]

Because Okonkwo rarely sees beyond the surface meaning
of words and phrases, he does not understand the difference between obeying the Earth's messenger stated in the first sentence
and becoming her messenger implied in the following proverb.
Hence, his confusion about the meaning of the two statements
shows that Okonkwo is too literal rather than analytical in his
interpretations.

In a recent interview when speaking of Okonkwo's character in general and his killing of Ikemefuna in particular,
Achebe commented upon the protagonist's literalism thus:

> . . . Okonkwo is a single-minded person who accepts
> what he feels as the norms of his community and acts in
> a kind of literal-minded way. He is not going to be
> swayed by any other considerations other than those
> he understands his community stands for. And he is
> right. But his community is always ready at the mo-
> ment of crisis to bend a little, whereas someone like
> Okonkwo, who is literal-minded, will not bend to the
> community. For example, when he kills Ikemefuna, his
> community condemns the act. But for Okonkwo, some-

body has to kill him because the society *says* he should
be killed.[11]

Here, in this analysis of Okonkwo's literal-mindedness,
Achebe asserts that all societies have their negative and positive
qualities, and the unthinking people of these societies, who
make no distinction between the bad and the good, can do ir-
reparable harm to their communities.   The ritualistic killing of
Ikemefuna and the abandonment of the twins are two of these
negative acts, both mandatory in the Ibo system, yet both irra-
tional and inhumane.   However, Okonkwo never once questions the ethics of either practice.   Societies themselves, Achebe
implies, sometimes plant the seeds that can hasten their own
disintegration, and the Ibo society is no exception.   And such
negative seeds placed into the hands of a literal-minded man
like Okonkwo, who takes it upon himself to champion *all* the
values of Ibo tribal life without careful analysis or questions, can
indeed become very destructive to the fabric of society.

In holding the defects of the Ibo value system up to analysis, Achebe does not overlook the numerous shortcomings of
the European value system exported to Nigeria by the British
and imposed upon the indigenous people.   Although some critics hold that Achebe in the manner of a historian makes no
value judgment upon either social system or dogmatic assertion
upon which system is better or worse,[12] the European system
does come in for a sounder thrashing than the Ibo system, despite the fact that Achebe is not as extreme as other African writers in his analysis.

When Okonkwo inadvertently kills a kinsman, Ezeudu's
son, he is exiled from Umuofia and sent to Mbanta, the home of
his mother's kinsmen, in keeping with tribal law.   This inadvertent act by Okonkwo allows Achebe to discuss the consequences
of the white missionaries' coming to Umuofia during
Okonkwo's absence and the falling apart of the clan hastened by
their coming.   It, likewise, allows Achebe to demonstrate his
skill in establishing an inner conflict within the protagonist: that
is, Okonkwo's desire to carry out the terms of his exile and his
equal desire, at the same time, to return to Umuofia and rid his
clan of the white man.   Moreover, the novelist uses the protagonist's accidental commission of a crime and a seven-year absence as an important structural device to divide Okonkwo from
his people and to emphasize the profound changes that take
place in the interim.

During the period of Okonkwo's exile, Christian missionaries and British government officials arrive in the Umuofian
village. With their guile, self-righteousness, and feelings of su-
periority, they first appeal to the outcasts or nonconformists of
Ibo society. One of these nonconformists is Okonkwo's oldest
son, Nwoye, who has become disturbed about the senseless
killing of his adopted brother, Ikemefuna, and about the tribal
custom of abandoning new-born twins to die in the Evil Forest.
Of Nwoye's reaction to the missionaries' appeal, the narrator
comments that

> It was not the mad logic of the Trinity that captivated
> him. He did not understand it. It was the poetry of the
> new religion, something felt in the marrow. The hymn
> about brothers who sat in darkness and in fear seemed
> to answer a vague and persistent question that haunted
> his young soul—the question of the twins crying in the
> bush and the question of Ikemefuna who was killed. He
> felt a relief within as the hymn poured into his
> parched soul. The words of the hymn were like a drop
> of frozen rain melting on the dry palate of the panting
> earth.[13]

Some critics have commented upon the objective manner
in which Achebe presents the methods and techniques of the
white missionaries and the British government officials.[14] Another, in a similar vein, has noted the balanced treatment given
to both the strengths and defects of the African and European
value systems.[15] Still another has gone so far as to assert that
Achebe sees the new dispensation as something desirable.[16] In
advancing these views, these commentators have apparently
overlooked the sarcasm and satire that Achebe uses in describing
the guile of Mr. Brown and the overzealousness of Reverend
James Smith, the white missionaries, who come to the
Umuofian village in Okonkwo's absence to free the natives
from their "ignorance" and superstition. In describing Reverend
James Smith's religious zeal and superior bearing, for example,
the reader is told that

> Mr. Smith was greatly distressed by the ignorance
> which many of his flock showed even in such things as
> the Trinity and the Sacraments. It only showed that
> they were seeds sown on a rocky soil. Mr. Brown had
> thought of nothing but numbers. He should have known
> that the kingdom of God did not depend on large
> crowds. Our Lord Himself stressed the importance of
> fewness. To fill the Lord's holy temple with an idola-

> trous crowd clamoring for signs was a folly of everlast-
> ing consequence. Our Lord used the whip only once in
> His life—to drive the crowd away from the Church.[17]

It is true that Achebe also assigns to Okonkwo, the protagonist,
many excesses, but he does not delineate these excesses through
the literary device of sarcasm as he does in the cases of Mr.
Brown and Reverend Smith. Again, during the course of the
narrative when Mr. Brown's techniques in winning new converts to the new dispensation are described, the audience is ap-
prised through the literary devices of satire and sarcasm. "Mr.
Brown preached against such excesses of zeal," the omniscient
narrator informs the reader, "and so Mr. Brown came to be respected even by the clan, because he trod softly on its faith."[18] To
be sure, this passage can be interpreted to mean that Mr. Brown's
moderation stands in direct opposition to Reverend Smith's in-
temperance. However, upon a careful reading of the narrative,
it becomes clear that Achebe is demonstrating how the two
white missionaries used different means to achieve the same
ends: that is, to subvert the values of the indigenous culture.
Realizing that a frontal attack on the religion of the clan will not
succeed, Mr. Brown chooses instead to build a school in which to
indoctrinate the natives with European values.

The missionaries and British government officials could
not have succeeded had not some of the indigenous people co-
operated with their tactics. Some of the latter, for example, were
given "lucrative" positions in the government, where they co-
operated in oppressing their own people. It is revealing, for example, that when Okonkwo is arrested and jailed for destroying
the local church, the unduly harsh suffering he receives, though
emanating from British society, actually comes from the hands
of one of his own people, the hated court messenger. This messenger, who is the archetype of the assimilated indigenous person, shaves and knocks Okonkwo's and his men's heads together in a humiliating manner without any sense of remorse.
In fact, he disallows them even the elementary courtesies accorded human beings: that is, the right to get a drink of water or
to go out into the bush to relieve themselves. Of the missionaries' success in building new schools and winning new converts
such as the inhumane court messenger to their way of life, the
narrator states in a sarcastic tone:

> And it was not long before the people began to say that
> the white man's medicine was quick in working. Mr.

> Brown's school produced quick results. A few months in
> it were enough to make one a court messenger or even a
> court clerk. Those who stayed longer became teachers:
> and from Umuofia laborers went forth into the Lord's
> vineyard. New churches were established in the sur-
> rounding villages and a few schools with them. From
> the very beginning religion and education went hand in
> hand.[19]

Near the end of the novel, Okonkwo, the protagonist, stands
alone in his attempt to rid the clan of western influences. For
example, when the court messenger arrives to break up a meeting of the clan, Okonkwo in a moment of fury and an act of des-
peration beheads him but finds no support for his actions from
his own people. Then he kills himself, an indication that the
"things" alluded to in the title of the novel have irrevocably
fallen apart. The other characters seem to sense the futility of
fighting off the converging forces that cannot now be diverted.
These forces include not only the white man's firm determination to rule and to impose his values upon the Ibos by any
means necessary, supported by troops and the gun, but also the
oppression of the outcasts and nonconformists within the indigenous culture. Add to these forces the naïveté of the Ibo people in assessing and comprehending the motives of the British
colonialists, and therein lies the making of an unsolvable
dilemma. Even Achebe himself in speaking of the Ibo people
has stated that "basically we're timid people. Not only timid, we
wallow in self-deception."[20]

When the forces of history all converge in chapter twenty-
five of the novel, Achebe puts the reader into the mind of the
white District Commissioner, the archetype of the European
administrator, who becomes an instant "expert" on Africa.
Viewing the mores of Ibo society from a narrow perspective, the
commissioner demonstrates his ethnocentric bias in his inability
to understand the human dimensions of Okonkwo's fate and in
his use of the phrase "Primitive Tribes" in the title of his proposed book about African history. For example, when
Okonkwo's body is found hanging from a tree, Obierika and
members of the clan refuse to bury him in keeping with tribal
custom. Rather, Obierika requests the District Commissioner to
ask his men to perform the burial rites, since they are strangers.
Lacking the capacity to perceive the significance and human
dimensions of Okonkwo's tragedy, the commissioner does order
his chief messenger to take down Okonkwo's body "and bring it

and all these people to the court." However, because he sees everything from a narrow western perspective, the District Commissioner, who is a symbol of tribal disintegration and administrative oppression, views Okonkwo's death only as an opportunity to give a pointless lesson on European etiquette:

> In the many years in which he had toiled to bring civilization to different parts of Africa he had learned a number of things. One of them was that a District Commissioner must never attend to details as cutting a hanged man from the tree. Such attention would give the natives a poor opinion of him. In the book which he planned to write he would stress that point.[21]

Hence, Okonkwo's death and the District Commissioner's insensitive attitude toward the African way of life intensify the reader's awareness of the demoralizing effects that colonialism wreaked upon the indigenous people of Nigeria. This same insensitivity and ethnocentrism are again displayed when the commissioner tells of his intention to write only one paragraph about Okonkwo's death and, by extension, the dying of the Ibo way of life in his proposed book about the African experience, *The Pacification of the Primitive Tribes of the Lower Niger*.

The irony in the commissioner's statement is too obvious for the reader to ignore. Not only does the commissioner plan to de-emphasize the death of Ibo culture by writing only one paragraph about Okonkwo's death, but also the Umuofian clansmen stood by and allowed that history to be diminished without putting up any real resistance. Only Okonkwo escapes the final irony of the situation through taking his own life, an act especially horrible within the African context.

In summary, Chinua Achebe's novel, *Things Fall Apart*, is an extremely well-written work demonstrating the author's narrative skill and technique. The work details the conflict in values between the old order represented by Okonkwo and his clan, and the values of the new order represented by Christianity and British colonialism. In the novel, the Ibos are initially pictured as deriving peace and contentment from rural life and from the unity of the Umuofian clan before the arrival of the Europeans. After the latter's advent, the peace and unity of the clan are disturbed as a result of the imported ideas forced upon them by the British missionaries and government officials. Then the clan falls apart in spite of Okonkwo's final abortive attempt to stem the tide, and the new order represented by the white man's Christianity and way of life seems to triumph.

Serious readers of this work have pondered why the new order with its emphasis on an entirely different set of values seems to triumph over the values of the old order which were even more legitimate and suited to the Ibo people. The answer is admittedly not a simple one. However, Achebe as the consummate intellectual dared not distort historical events even within a fictional medium. Rather, he decided to present these facts about the conflicts in culture honestly and truthfully. After all, what is literature anyway except fictionalized truth? This is the way it happened, Achebe seems to imply, when Africa met Europe in this tragic encounter. As literary historian, he is neither romanticizing the past not glorifying the present. However, he is much more condemnatory, in the novel, of the British colonialists who tampered with and, in many instances, subverted the Ibo value system and the way of life than he is upon the unsuspecting indigenous people, who, because of their naïveté and blind trust in strangers, caused their own countrymen to develop what Achebe himself has called a "crisis of the soul." Just recently, for example, in speaking of the effects of Europeanization upon the young intellectuals of his generation, the novelist commented:

> . . . what I think is the basic problem of a new African country like Nigeria is what you might call a 'crisis' in the soul. We have been subjected—we have subjected ourselves too—to this period during which we have accepted everything alien as good and practically everything local or native as inferior. I could give you illustrations of when I was growing up, the attitude of our parents, the Christian parents, to Nigerian dances, to Nigerian handicrafts: and the whole society during the period began to look down on itself . . . and this was a very bad thing: and we . . . still haven't got over this period. I can give . . . the example of the boy in my wife's class who said he wouldn't write about harmattan because it was 'bush.' You see, he would rather write about winter.[22]

From his comments about the harmful effects of Europeanization upon his own people, and from the sarcastic and ironical way in which Achebe describes the tactics of the white missionaries and government officials in *Things Fall Apart*, it seems safe to conclude that this "crisis of the soul" left permanent scars upon the Ibo people and virtually destroyed and perverted their system of values.

Notes

[1] In addition to *Things Fall Apart* (1958), Achebe has written three novels, *No Longer at Ease* (1960), *Arrow of God* (1964), and *A Man of the People* (1964).

[2] Chinua Achebe, "The Role of the Writer in a New Nation," *Nigeria Magazine* No. 81 (June 1964), 157.

[3] For other points of view about the structure of *Things Fall Apart*, see Robert M. Wren, *Achebe's World: the Historical and Cultural Context of the Novel* (Washington, D.C.: Three Continents Press, Inc., 1980), pp. 23-26; Charles R. Larson, *The Emergence of African Fiction* (Bloomington, Indiana: Indiana University Press), pp. 30-63 and J. Dedenuola, "The Structure of Achebe's *Things Fall Apart*," *Nigeria Magazine* 103 (1969-1970), 638-669.

[4] Larson, p. 30.

[5] All reference to *Things Fall Apart* in this paper are to Chinua Achebe, *Things Fall Apart* (Greenwich, Connecticut: Fawcett Publications, Inc., 1959), p. 12—hereafter referred to as *Things Fall Apart*.

[6] *Things Fall Apart*, p. 17.

[7] Some critics regard *Things Fall Apart* as an epic and Okonkwo, the protagonist, as essentially heroic. See, for example, John Povey, "The Novels of Chinua Achebe" in *Introduction to Nigerian Literature*, ed. Bruce King (Lagos, Nigeria: Africana Publishing Co., 1971), p. 101 and David Cook, *African Literature: A Critical View* (London: Western Printing Services Ltd., 1977), pp. 66-67.

[8] Phyllis M. Martin and Patrick O'Meara, eds., *Africa* (Bloomington, Indiana: Indiana University Press, 1977), p. 340.

[9] *Things Fall Apart*, p. 66.

[10] *Things Fall Apart*, p. 64.

[11] Phanuel Akubueze Egejuru, *Towards African Literary Independence: A Dialogue with Contemporary African Writers* (Westport, Connecticut: Greenwood Press, 1980), pp. 134-124.

[12] Cook, p. 67.

[13] *Things Fall Apart*, p. 137.

[14] See Oladele Taiwo, *An Introduction to West African Literature* (London: The Trinity Press, 1967), p. 58 and Cook, pp. 67-68.

[15] See, for example, the discussion of the novel's general conclusion in the essay by Donald Weinstock and Cathy Ramadan, "Symbolic Structure in *Things Fall Apart*," *Critical Perspectives on Chinua Achebe*, eds. C. L. Innes and Bernth Lindfors (Washington, D.C.: Three Continents Press, 1978), p. 134.

[16] Larson, p. 61.

[17] *Things Fall Apart*, p. 169.

[18] *Things Fall Apart*, p. 163.

[19] *Things Fall Apart*, p. 166.

[20] John Agetua, "Interview with Professor Chinua Achebe on August 16, 1976" in *Critics on Chinua Achebe 1970-76* (Benin City, 1977).

[21] *Things Fall Apart*, p. 191.

[22] Wren, p. 16.

Rhythm and Narrative Method in Achebe's
Things Fall Apart

B. Eugene McCarthy

Before the publication of Chinua Achebe's *Things Fall Apart* in 1958, public awareness in the West of fiction from Africa was confined chiefly to white writers such as Doris Lessing, Alan Paton, or Nadine Gordimer. Thus Achebe's first novel, written in English, though he is himself a Nigerian of the Igbo people, was a notable event. More noteworthy was the fact that it was a very good novel and has become over the years probably the most widely read and talked abut African novel, overshadowing the efforts of other West African novelists as well as those of East and South Africa. Its reputation began high and has remained so, stimulating critical analysis in hundreds of articles, many books, and dissertations. Its story describes, whatever one may expect from its Yeatsian title, the life of a traditional Igbo rural village and the rise of one of its gifted leaders, Okonkwo, before colonization, and then observes the consequences for the village and the hero as they confront the beginnings of the colonial process. Achebe's subsequent three novels, more or less related but not sequential, *No Longer At Ease* (1960), *Arrow of God* (1964), and *Man of the People* (1966), though all respected, have not matched its success. Achebe's fiction established firmly that there is an African prose literature—poetry had probably been well known since Senghor in the 1940s—even when written in English. Not that there has not been debate over and criticism of *Things Fall Apart*, and from Achebe's standpoint a good deal of misunderstanding through refusal of readers to take its African character seriously; but as a recent study confirms he continues to be "the most widely read of contemporary African writers."[1] His first novel has been "as big a

factor in the formation of a young West African's picture of his
past and of his relation to it, as any of the still rather distorted
teachings of the pulpit and the primary school,"[2] and of course
he has influenced his fellow writers just as significantly in find-
ing their own subject matter and voice.

When beginning Chinua Achebe's novel *Things Fall
Apart*, readers are often struck by the simple mode of narration
and equally simple prose style, which critics have seen as
Achebe's desire to achieve an "English . . . colored to reflect the
African verbal style [with] stresses and emphases that would be
eccentric and unexpected in British or American speech."[3] He
reshapes English in order to imitate the "linguistic patterns of
his mother tongue," Igbo.[4] I would like, as a further means of
understanding this special quality of Achebe's prose, to propose a
way of reading and of understanding the novel through the concept of rhythm, within the oral tradition.

In the opening passage of the novel, the narrator's repetition of words and phrases, both verbatim and synonymous, and
his mode of emphasis and patterning suggest a deliberateness
and complexity well beyond the surface simplicity:

    A   a
Okonkwo *was* well known *throughout the nine*

        A a
villages and even beyond. His fame *rested on solid*

            A
personal achievements. As a young man of eighteen he

     a   B
had brought honour *to his village* by throwing

  C   C
Amalinze the Cat. Amalinze *was the great wrestler*

       D
who for seven years *was unbeaten, from Umuofia to*

        C
Mbaino. He was called the Cat *because his back would*

         C   A
never touch the earth. It was this man *that* Okonkwo

 B
threw *in a fight which the old men agreed was one of*

        E
the fiercest *since the founder of their town engaged a*

     E   D
spirit of the wild *for* seven days and seven nights.

The drums beat and the flutes sang and the
                                   C   E

spectators held their breath. Amalinze *was a* wily
               A   E

craftsman, but Okonkwo *was as* slippery *as a fish in*
         E

water. Every nerve and every muscle stood out *on their*

arms, on their backs and their thighs, and one almost
               E

heard them stretching to breaking point. *In the end*
   A   B   C
Okonkwo threw the Cat.[5]

    The narrator's repetitions in this passage are a technique of the traditional oral storyteller, sitting talking to a group of listeners (though he is not a *griot*, or oral historian).[6] For example, the subject "A" repeats four times, the modifier "a" repeats but varies to add meanings; other words, such as those about the intensity of the fight, likewise are repeated to emphasize their importance and to vary meanings. Walter Ong refines our understanding of oral thought and expression in prose by pointing out that the oral narrator's "thought must come into being in heavily rhythmic, balanced patterns, in repetitions and antitheses, in alliterations and assonances, in epithetic and other formulary expressions. . . ." Such primary devices for memory ("for rhythm aids recall") and communication simplify the story so that the listeners can grasp characters and events graphically and surely. More specifically, oral expression is "additive rather than subordinative," "aggregative rather than analytical," "redundant or 'copious,'" that is, "backlooping" by means of "redundancy, repetition of the just-said."[7] The additive and redundant elements are apparent in the above passage, when Achebe's narrator repeats a phrase, for example, "Amalinze the Cat," then carries it forward with new information. Once a name or event is introduced he proceeds by moving forward, then reaching back to repeat and expand, moving onward again, accumulating detail and elaborating: "well known" advances to "fame" and to "honour," just as "It was this man that Okonkwo threw" repeats what has gone before and underlines its importance. Karl H. Bottcher calls the narrator's method "afterthoughts,"[8] but Ong's "backlooping" conveys better the active methodology of the narrator.

The style is not "aggregative" for key epithets are not attached to characters, no doubt because the novel is written, not spoken. A more important departure from strict oral procedure is the narrator's distance from his characters and his reluctance to intrude his views, for as Ong tells us, empathy and participation are elements of orality, objectivity a consequence of writing.[9] For the most part the narrator reveals only what was done or said by others: "a fight which the *old men agreed* was one of the fiercest . . . ," "*it was said* that, when he slept . . . ," "he *seemed* to walk on springs, *as if.* . . ." We understand an apparent intrusion such as the following as reflecting not the narrator's bias but the way the people thought: "When Unoka died he had taken no title at all and he was heavily in debt. Any wonder then that his son Okonkwo was ashamed of him? Fortunately, among these people a man was judged according to his worth and not according to the worth of his father" (p. 6).

The patterning and repetition in Achebe's novel are characteristics of the self-conscious artistry of oral narrative performance, where plot moves by repetition and predictability. Harold Scheub argues the "centrality of repetition in oral narratives as a means of establishing rhythm."[10] Such rhythmic textures establish the narrative method as imitative of the African oral rather than the English "literary" tradition. Indeed rhythm is a quality at the heart of African culture. Léopold Sédar Senghor has written: "Rhythm is the architecture of being, the inner dynamic that gives it form, the pure expression of the life force." The dramatic interest of a work is not sustained, he writes, by "avoiding repetition as in European narrative . . . , [but] is born of repetition: repetition of a fact, of a gesture, of words that form a *leitmotiv*. There is always the introduction of a new element, variation of the repetition, unity in diversity."[11] In the text where he quotes this statement, Jahnheinz Jahn illustrates prose rhythms with a passage from Nigerian writer Amos Tutuola's *Palm-Wine Drinkard*: "The rhythmical kind of narrative in which the repetition intensifies the dramatic quality of the action makes Tutuola's story oral literature."[12]

As Robert Kellogg tells us, there are many sorts of rhythm, "phonic, metrical, grammatical, metaphoric, imagistic, thematic,"[13] and modern studies have argued that prose as well as verse has its rhythms, usually found first in syntax.[14] The repetitions of syntactic patterns of word and phrase underscore emphases (sometimes vocal) and stresses of meaning. Thus Roger

Fowler describes in passages from David Storey the syntactic repetitions by which "syntax becomes rhythmical" and finds "sen-
tence- and phase-rhythms" there like "'thickening, deepening,
then darkening'": "When syntax is repetitious, highlighting by
reiteration a small number of patterns," he argues, "a palpable
rhythm is established through the regularity of voice tunes."[15]
Such repetition is the most obvious stylistic feature we notice in
the passage from Achebe's novel. Syntactically, these repetitions
stress key words, often polysyllables in contrast to the predomi-
nating one or two syllable words, chiefly subject nouns, object
nouns, pronouns and modifiers of these nouns, and verbs, with
occasional stress on time or place. Though emphasis may be difficult to assess uniformly—e.g., "through the NINE villages," or
"through the NINE VILLAGES," or even possibly "through the
nine VILLAGES"—there are some evident emphases on subjects, objects, or verbs; for example, "In the end Okonkwo threw
the Cat" stresses all three. Parallelism enhances the repetitions
and strengthens the rhythms: the parallel subject-verb sentence
opening: "Okonkwo was" with "fame rested," or "Amalinze
was" with "he was" with "It was." In the third (unquoted) paragraph, the parallel repetitions become insistent, as the verbs become increasingly active: "he was tall," "he breathed," "he slept,"
"he walked," "he seemed to walk," "He was going," "he did
pounce," "he had," and finally, "He had no patience. . . ." Allit-
eration too accents these repetitions: "called" and "Cat"; "fight,"
"fiercest," and "founder"; "Spirit," "seven," and "seven." One
may even discern a distinct metrical rhythm in some lines, such
as, "The drums beat and the flutes sang and the spectators held
their breath," which could be marked, short, long, long; short,
short, long, long, and so on. The third paragraph summarizes
with a strongly trochaic, blues-like line: "That was many years
ago, twenty years or more," but the near domination of metric
regularity chants to "and during this time, Okonkwo's fame. . . ."
If there is such a thing as a dominant meter in prose (English is
considered to be naturally iambic),[16] Achebe's prose would seem
to be largely anapestic: "It was this/ man that Okon/kwo threw/
in a fight/ which the old/ men agreed/ was one/ of the fierc/est
since the found/er of their town/ engaged a spir/it of the wild/
for sev/en days/ and sev/en nights," ending with a series of four
iambs. Note another anapestic line: "Every nerve/ and every
mus/cle stood out/ on their arms/ on their backs/ and their
thighs." The point here is not to scan the lines but to shadow

the rhythmical quality of the prose, more markedly rhythmical than traditional English prose, closer to an oral African quality.

I will explore now further levels of rhythm in the novel, moving from the stylistic to the structural, and then to the thematic, for not only the style but the entire narrative method can be considered rhythmical. Critics have mentioned the structuring of events in the novel in terms of rhythm. According to David Carroll, "the narrator then moves from this larger rhythm of the generations to the rhythm of the seasons, to Okonkwo and his sons repairing the walls; . . . yet the compassionate narrative voice seems to establish another rhythm, contrapuntal to Okonkwo's success."[17] S. O. Iyasere says, "Against the joyfully harmonic rhythm of this event [the locusts], the withdrawn, controlled formalism of the judgment of the *egwugu* stands in sharp relief. By juxtaposing these events, Achebe orchestrates the modulating rhythms of Umoufia."[18] The structural tightness of the novel has been demonstrated by critics such as Robert Wren on the novel as a whole,[19] and Karl Bottcher on the narrator's voice and other stylistic techniques.[20] The narrative procedure that we see in the opening passages, involving a regular introduction of new materials, a little at a time, awaiting further amplification, is similar to African polymetric rhythms in which various meters are heard simultaneously, though not introduced at one time.[21] This is not a rhythm of percussive stress or beat, but an accentuation by word, phrase or theme. As our awareness is sharpened to the introduction of new materials—the "additive" element of orality— we become aware of the multiple rhythms at work: words that emulate the "redundant" aspect of orality by early or late repetition (e.g. "breath," "seven"), themes that are briefly expanded or developed later (e.g. fierceness, wrestling), and those such as *masculine* and *feminine* that evolve slowly but consistently. We thus become more conscious of the process of development of words, phrases, and themes, and are less likely to overemphasize one and miss another. We will also see that the narrative makes increasingly evident a connection between these rhythmic elements of style and form and the basic rhythm of clan life, with the result that rhythm becomes significant thematically to Okonkwo's response to clan life and to the ultimate breaking of that life. I will sketch the pattern of the thirteen chapters of Part One to show how the narrative is laid before us, like pieces of a complex puzzle that slowly reveal coherence.

In Chapter One we meet Okonkwo as a man of great achievement and greater potential, and we see the heritage of his father the failure, a heritage Okonkwo wishes to flee. But as Okonkwo hastens to achieve his goals he inadvertently becomes involved with the hostage, the boy Ikemefuna whom the narrator refers to as "doomed" and "ill-fated," though we are unsure why at this point. The pacing of Chapter Two is particularly suggestive of the narrative method used thereafter in the novel. Set in three parts the chapter begins with Okonkwo, about to go to bed hearing "a clear overtone of tragedy in the crier's voice." We drift briefly from that motif to hear lore of the night before we continue the episode of Ikemefuna's arrival in Umuofia into the care of Okonkwo. The second part turns abruptly to the character of Okonkwo, "dominated by fear, the fear of failure and of weakness," specifically of being thought an "agbala," a woman, or a man with no titles, like his father. "And so Okonkwo was ruled by one passion—to hate everything that his father Unoka had loved. One of those things was gentleness and another was idleness" (p. 10). When in the third part the chapter returns to details of Ikemefuna's arrival—as Bottcher says, "the point of departure is resumed almost word by word"[22]—w e have in a nutshell the whole novel: Okonkwo's passions, hatred of weakness or womanliness, his success and strengths, his connection with the hostage, and the overtones of tragedy.

The three parts of Chapter Two offer an episodic advancement of the plot, both adding to what has been mentioned and reflecting on the parts to which they are juxtaposed for commentary and contrast, as well as introducing new materials, all in the oral-rhythmic process of addition of new and amplification of old themes. Chapter Three, also of three parts (though the chapters vary generally from one to four parts), begins with Agbala, not the scornful title of "woman" but the Oracle whose priestess people visit "to discover what the future held . . . or to consult the spirits of their departed father" (p. 12). Agbala had once told Unoka why he was a failure. Now, to overcome the disadvantages of a useless father, Okonkwo visits not Agbala but, more practically, a wealthy man for a loan of yams to start his own farm. Part Three then reverses the trend of the story thus far, for Okonkwo fails, and establishes the possibility of things going badly to the point of suicide. "The year had gone mad," and all his seed yams have been destroyed. One man hangs himself, but Okonkwo survives because of "his inflexible will."

Having established Okonkwo's direction, the narrator wishes to expand the context of the novel and offer several correctives, for the implications of the incident of Okonkwo's "survival" are not resolved until Chapter Four. "'Looking at a king's mouth,' said an old man, 'one would think he never sucked at his mother's breast.' He was talking about Okonkwo" (p. 19), who had indeed forgotten his maternal life, and preferred "to kill a man's spirit" by calling him "woman." Okonkwo's fear of weakness is here qualified as specifically antifeminine: "To show affection as a sign of weakness," so he beats his hostage, and in the next part beats one of his wives in violation of the Week of Peace dedicated to the Goddess Ani, an evil act that "'can ruin the whole clan. The earth goddess whom you have insulted may refuse to give us her increase and we shall all perish'" (p. 22).

The importance of the feminine element in the culture could be overlooked because of the emphasis Okonkwo places on masculine virtues and achievements for which he is justly celebrated. But the novel steadfastly points to the centrality of the feminine.[23] Okonkwo's masculine sensibility terrorizes his son Nwoye whom he wishes to be "a great farmer and a great man" (p. 23), and enhances his affection for the already manly Ikemefuna, who significantly entertains such "womanly" traits as telling (p. 24) and hearing (p. 42) folk tales. Okonkwo's emphasis on "his inflexible will" as the cause of his survival is corrected here when the narrator explicitly states, "the personal dynamism required to counter the forces of these extremes of weather would be far too great for the human frame" (p. 24).

One new element is introduced in this chapter, the concern with customs. Since Okonkwo had violated the custom of the Week of Peace, the discussion is appropriate, but its importance here is in revealing that the clan's customs are not absolute: "the punishment for breaking the Peace of Ani had become very mild in their clan." The men mock those clans who do not alter customs as they see fit: "they lack understanding." If we think too much on change as things-falling-apart, we are apt to miss the ameliorative process of change which is inherent in the clan. Throughout the story several old men and some young men ponder the sanity of customs, such as the particularly agonizing one of killing twins and we are conscious that eventually it too would be changed. Desire for change, founded in emotional distress, is what brings Nwoye to Christianity for solace.

Chapter Five returns to another feast of the Earth Goddess to elaborate her position. The "source of all fertility[,] Ani played a greater part in the life of the people than any other deity. She was the ultimate judge of morality and conduct" (p. 26). During her feast, for which the local women inscribe themselves and their huts with detailed patterns, and to which visitors come from the motherland (and reportedly spoil the children!), the violence of Okonkwo once more erupts. He rages that a tree has been killed—"As a matter of fact the tree was very much alive"—and then shoots at his wife, the one who (as we later learn) had left her husband out of admiration for Okonkwo's excellence as a wrestler. The implications of this wild act of shooting eventually become clear for though there was no formal violation of the harvest festival, Okonkwo here mishandles a gun as he will later do in fatefully killing a boy.

The remainder of Chapter Five is filled with the wonderful power of the drums, like the rhythmic pulse of the heart of the clan, sounding insistently behind the action—"Just then the distant beating of drums began to reach them" (p. 30), "The drums were still beating, persistent and unchanging" (p. 31), "In the distance the drums continued to beat" (p. 32). They are a pulse countered only by Okonkwo's roaring at his daughter Ezinma who he wished were a boy. At this point rhythm takes on thematic dimensions as the narrator contrasts Okonkwo's eccentric or asymmetrical behavior with the rhythmic spirit of the clan. The significance of the drum beat is amplified in the following chapter (Six) where the chief entertainment of the clan, wrestling, takes place on the *ilo*, the village circle, a dramatic space where the central physical and cultural acts of the people occur (recall the spiritual "dark, endless *space* in the presence of Agbala," p. 12). Later (Chapter Ten) judgments are passed there on major legal cases, and finally (Chapter Twenty-Three) when the clan is disrupted and the imagery is of coldness and ashes, no acts take place: "the village *ilo* where they had always gathered for a moon-play was empty" (p. 139). Our attention is drawn inexorably to the *ilo* by the drums so that by the time the celebration begins, we watch the people drawn in every sense together by the drums, for the drummers are literally "possessed by the spirit of the drums" (p. 33) and their "frantic rhythm was . . . the very heart-beat of the people" (pp. 35-36). Rhythm is central. We are to see this celebration as the focal dramatic act of the dramatic space which is the center of the people—harmonic life—as if we as visitors to the clan must see at least once what rhythm means in its fullest articulation, must be reminded what it was like when, as the novel opened, Okonkwo threw the Cat, and when now, in almost exact repetition for Okonkwo, for his wife, for the clan, "The muscles on their arms and their thighs and on their backs stood out and twitched, . . .

> Has he thrown a hundred Cats?
> He has thrown four hundred Cats.   (p. 36)

This is the cultural center of the novel—the *ilo* becomes a metaphor for the dramatic space of the novel, the cultural locus upon which Okonkwo performs, first as wrestler, then as tragic actor. In *Achebe's World* Robert Wren also emphasizes this chapter: the novel's twenty-five chapters "are upon closer analysis divided into four groups of six chapters each, with one pivotal chapter, XIII, where Okonkwo accidentally kills Ezeudu's son and must flee."[24] Wren goes on to note that Part One actually "has two six-chapter units plus the pivotal chapter." The stress is on Chapter Six, the drum chapter, as a center of this Part (for with Seven we move to the killing of Ikemefuna), so there is an imbalance with Chapter Thirteen: the "alternating chapters show Okonkwo in crisis": VII, IX, XI and XIII.[25]

Hereafter in Chapter Seven as things begin to break down, we can view Okonkwo's eventual tragedy as a violation of this harmony. We notice how he stands obnoxious and restless against the festival of drums: "never . . . enthusiastic over feasts," he picks a quarrel over the "dead" tree, shoots at his wife, jealously sees Obierika's son become wrestling hero instead of his son (p. 34). Playwright and critic Wole Soyinka tells us that a person must constantly attempt to bridge the gulf between the area of earthly existence and the existence of deities, ancestors and the unborn by "sacrifices, the rituals, the ceremonies of appeasement to those cosmic powers which lie guardian to the gulf. . . . Tragedy, in Yoruba traditional drama, is the anguish of this severance, the fragmentation of essence from self."[26] Achebe's narrator underscores the same sense of cosmic responsibility in Chapter Thirteen: "A man's life from birth to death was a series of transition rites which brought him nearer and nearer to his ancestors" (p. 85). Achebe's is not Yoruba fiction but Soyinka's description gives, I think, an important clue to Okonkwo's tragedy: separation from what the clan adheres to as value, specifically here the rhythmic center of life.

In Chapter Seven the actions run together without division and there is a symbolic heightening of word and action as if we are continuing from the previous chapter with specially meaningful narrative. As Okonkwo told Nwoye and Ikemefuna "masculine stories of violence and bloodshed . . . they sat in darkness," a terrible symbolic image, especially in contrast to Nwoye's love of "stories his mother used to tell," folk tales of mercy and pity at which "he warmed himself" as Vulture did in the tale (p. 38). (Note that Okonkwo almost inadvertently remembers in detail his mother's folk tale, p. 53.) Then the locusts came, destroyers late identified with "the white man" (p. 97). Okonkwo is warned "to have nothing to do with" killing Ikemefuna, for "He calls you his father." But then—in the suddenly symbolic phrasing of the narrator, "in the narrow line in the heart of the forest," the narrow line between obedience to the Oracle or obedience to humanity and the advice of Obierika, a line which crossed either way would be destructive—"Dazed with fear, Okonkwo drew his matchet and cut him down. He was afraid of being thought weak" (p. 43). And Nwoye, knowing what his father had done, felt "something . . . give way inside him," just as he did before when he "heard the voice of an infant crying in the thick forest," thrown there to die in a pot. "It descended on him again, this feeling, when his father walked in, that night after killing Ikemefuna" (p. 43).

The rhythm of the narrative does not end here with the broken rhythm of Okonkwo's life. The style continues much as before; Wilfred Cartey observes Achebe's repetition of images in Part Two: "When the rain finally came, it was in large, solid drops of frozen water which the people called 'the nuts of the water of heaven'" (p. 92); similarly, Nwoye feels Christianity "like the drops of frozen rain melting on the dry palate of the panting earth" (p. 104).[27] In the first chapter of Part Two, Okonkwo is introduced through a kind of repetition or review of his life from childhood to manhood, for the purpose of renewing his way of seeing. The first truth he is taught is the role of the female; not only has Okonkwo committed a female crime of inadvertently killing a boy when his gun exploded, but his penalty is seven (the number we say in the opening passage) years exile in his motherland:

Can you tell me, Okonkwo, why it is that one of the

commonest names we give our children is Nneka, or
            A
'Mother is Supreme'? *We all know that a man is the*

head of the family and his wives do his bidding. A
            B   C
child belongs to its father *and his family and* not to its
                                        B
mother *and her family.* A man belongs to his father-
            C
land *and* not to his motherland. *And yet we say*
            A
Nneka. . . .

    You do not know the answer? So you see that you
                                              B
are a child. . . . Listen to me. . . . It's true that a child -

belongs to its father. *But when a father beats his*
            D
child, it seeks sympathy in its mother's hut. A man
B
belongs to his fatherland *when things are good and life*

is sweet. But when there is sorrow and bitterness he
            D   D
finds refuge in his motherland. *Your* mother is there to

protect you. *She is buried there. And that is why we*
            A
say that mother is supreme.   (p. 94)

In spite of the additive qualities of the motherland (D) as sympathy, refuge and protection, Okonkwo's course is clear cut: he will eschew the feminine and, unchanged, act towards others as he acted before. Though the rhythms of the clan are by no mean perfect, he refuses to respond to their fulfillment and direction, and refers later to these years as "wasted." "He cannot see the wise balance," Ravenscroft writes, "in the tribal arrangement by which the female principle is felt to be simultaneously weak and sustaining."[28] But the newly introduced element of the white men will alter his course much further. As subtle as the colonists' entrance is the narrator's addition of a feature at a time: at first an unknown, the white men become a joke, then formidable missionaries, then government, then place of judgment, then "religion and trade and government" and prison (p. 123).

For all the disruption wrought by the whites, Christianity is not itself necessarily bad. The customs of the clan, which had been considered by some to be foolish or baneful and would in time be altered as others had, are accelerated to change by Christianity. Nwoye accepts the religion primarily because it answers a felt need. "It was the poetry of the new religion, something felt in the marrow," like the folk tales he loved earlier. "The hymn about brothers who sat in darkness and in fear seemed to answer a vague and persistent question that haunted his young soul [just as he and Ikemefuna had sat in darkness listening to Okonkwo's tales of the past]—the question of the twins crying in the bush and the question of Ikemefuna who was killed" (p. 104). Christianity speaks directly to Nwoye's needs, not in rational or doctrinal terms but in mercy and comfort of spirit. Nor does it seem that his reaction is destructive of any of the prior values of the clan; certainly Ikemefuna was a richly responsive human, lacking neither masculine strength nor feminine mercy and the only counter to Nwoye's inclinations was Okonkwo's insistence on masculinity. Christianity itself is greatly varied by its practitioners the missionaries, for whereas Brown (midway between black and white) actually tried to understand African belief and respond with some sensitivity to the people (he is still obtuse: "a frontal attack . . . would not succeed," p. 128), another, with the nondescript name of Smith, "saw things as black and white. And black was evil" (p. 130). Such dogmatic cruelty had not appeared in the novel until this missionary; and of course he succeeds because he is inflexible and tyrannical, while complex persons of compassion are overcome or bypassed.

> Seven years *was a long time* to be away *from one's* clan. *A man's* place *was not always there, waiting for him. As soon as he* left, *someone else rose and filled it. The* clan *was like a lizard; if it* lost its tail it *soon grew another.*
>
> Okonkwo knew *these things. He* knew *that he had* lost *his* place *among the nine masked spirits who administered justice in the* clan. *He* had lost *the chance to lead his warlike* clan *against the new religion, which, he was told, had gained ground. He* had lost *the years in which he might have taken the* highest titles *in the* clan. *But some of these* losses *were not irreparable. He was determined that his return should*

be marked by his people. He would return with a flour-
ish, and regain the seven wasted years.

Even in his first year of exile he had begun to plan
for his return. The first thing he would do would be to
rebuild his compound on a more magnificent scale. He
would build a bigger barn than he had before and he
would build huts for two new wives. Then he would
show his wealth by initiating his sons in the 'ozo' soci-
ety. Only the really great men in the clan were able to
do this. Okonkwo saw clearly the high esteem in
which he would be held, and he saw himself taking
the highest title in the land.   (p. 121)

The rhythms are clearly evident with the beat of key words and
tenses and voices: "he knew" (twice), "he had lost" (three times),
and so on to "he would return," "he would build," "he would
show," "he would be held," and "he saw." One·of the peculiar
effects of this repetition is that "he" is doing all the acting and
thinking so that the repetitions advance with very little return
to the beginning for elaboration. The "redundancy" lacks the element of "addition." Okonkwo marches forward, dreaming, not
reflecting, not in fact building upon the prior words and
thoughts. His mind works from knowing in truth to seeing in
fantasy, from knowledge of loss to determination to overcome
and excel. The repetitions mirror the stress between Okonkwo's
linear mentality and the clan's circular, rhythmic mode of repetition. For Okonkwo personally nothing has changed at home:
he curses his son Nwoye from the family and wishes Ezinma
were a boy, "She understood things so perfectly" (p. 122). So-
cially, however, outside Okonkwo's mind, there is now the new
religion, trade, government; and everyone knew the white man
"'has put a knife on the things that held us together and we
have fallen apart'" (pp. 124-125).

The rhythmic coherence of the novel is sustained through
to the end, at least when the narrator is describing the actions of
the clan. The words of the District Commissioner, however, or
words describing his actions, appear to be syntactically and philo-
sophically different. For instance, in the final chapter we read
the complex sentence:

When the District Commissioner arrived at
Okonkwo's compound at the head of an armed band of
soldier and court messengers he found a small crowd of
men sitting wearily in the obi. He commanded them to
come outside, and they obeyed without a murmur.
(p. 146)

The sentences are "subordinative" and sequential in narration of facts—this happened and then that—not at all in the "additive" rhythmic manner of accumulation of detail by repetition.[29] We are confronted by the difference between his speech and the clan's speech when the Commissioner complains to himself, "one of the most infuriating habits of these people was their love of superfluous words," for redundancy or copiousness is indeed one of the marks of oral speech. Rhythmic language follows as Obierika and his fellows approach Okonkwo's body hanging from a tree:

> *There was a* small bush *behind Okonkwo's* compound. *The only opening into this* bush *from the* compound *was a little* round hole *in the red-earth* wall *through which fowls went in and out in their endless search for food. The* hole *would not let a man through. It was to this* bush *that Obierika led the Commissioner and his men. They skirted round the* compound, *keeping close to the* wall. *The only sound they made was with their feet as they crushed dry leaves.*

The passage features assonance of the "o" to depict the "round hole," the now-familiar parallelism, repetition, specificity of detail and images, and continual expansion of the scene by repetition and addition. The verb "to be" dominates the sentences— "There was," "the opening . . . was," "it was"—and the weight of meaning is carried by objects, "bush," "compound," "hole," as if one's actions are relatable chiefly to stable poles of identification in the village rather than to one's personal activities.[30] The monosyllabic detail of the words quoted above gives them a symbolic tone, as if that little hole were the impossible fissure through which Okonkwo had passed by suicide into non-existence. The rhythmic phrasing stands sharply against the closing words of the Commissioner which are again logical and process-oriented, analytical, unsuperfluous, and non-African, with weight on verbs: he "arrived," "found," "commanded . . . and they obeyed." His arrogant dismissal of Okonkwo's story as deserving a bare paragraph in his book is mirrored in the straight-forward, one-dimensional prose.

The style of the novel and its structure thus draw attention to the exquisite tension between traditional English prose and the unique African and/or Igbo quality Achebe has created; it is, as Lloyd Brown says, "a total cultural experience, . . . the embodiment of its civilization."[31] Achebe himself is keenly aware of this quality of African style, as he points out in a passage from a Fulani creation myth: "You notice . . . how in the second section . . . we have that phrase *became too proud* coming back again and again like the recurrence of a dominant beat in rhythmic music?"[32]   In a discussion of his own prose, he illustrates "how I approach the use of English":

> *'I want one of my sons to join these people and be my eyes there. If there is nothing in it you will come back. But if there is something there you will bring home my share. The world is like a Mask, dancing. If you want to see it well you do not stand in one place. My spirit tells me that those who do not befriend the white man today will be saying* had we known *tomorrow.'*
>
> *Now supposing I had put it another way. Like this for instance:*
>
> *'I am sending you as my representative among these people—just be on the safe side in case the new religion develops. One has to move with the times or else one is left behind. I have a hunch that those who fail to come to terms with the white man may well regret their lack of foresight.'*[33]

Though Achebe does not spell out the differences between these passages, he seems fully conscious that the repetition of the "if" clauses creates that quality of rhythm which is missing in the "English" version, the metaphorical phrasing which, we should observe, issued in a colloquial rather than philosophical or proverbial sense. Rhythm, as Achebe seems well aware, thus can range from a stress within a phrase or sentence, to the structuring principle of a paragraph, to the form of an entire work. Through such a reading we may learn about the nature of rhythm and orality, and about the form of the novel, but especially we may better see the unique English Achebe has created and realize its African tone in order "to understand another whose language" one, as a non-African, "does not speak."[34]

Notes

[1] C. L. Innes and Bernth Lindfors, eds., *Critical Perspectives on Chinua Achebe* (Washington, D.C.: Three Continents Press, 1978), p. 1.

[2] Ibid., p. 5, quoting from *TLS* in 1965.

[3] John Povey, "The English Language of the Contemporary African Novel," *Critique* XI, 3 (1969), 93.

[4] Ihechukwu Madubuike, "Achebe's Ideas on African Literature," *New Letters* 40, 4 (1974), 87.

[5] Chinua Achebe, *Things Fall Apart* (London: Heinemann, 1958), p. 3. All subsequent quotations from the text are from this edition. Note: the word "men" above is written "man" in the text, which seems inconsistent with the referent "founder of *their* town."

[6] Meki Nzewi, "Ancestral Polyphony," *African Arts* 11, 4 (1978), 94: "But Chinua does not see a link between the modern Igbo novelist and the traditional storyteller." According to Professor Chidi Ikonne of Harvard University the narrator is not a *griot* (from private conversation). Yet Kofi Awoonor, *The Breast of the Earth* (Garden City, New York: Doubleday, 1976), p. 257, adds, there is a "straight-forward simplicity about the language . . . that recalls the raconteur's voice."

[7] Walter J. Ong, S.J., *Orality and Literacy* (London: Methuen, 1982), pp. 34, 37-40. Ong says Achebe's *No Longer at Ease* "draws directly on Ibo oral tradition . . . [providing] instances of thought patterns in orally educated characters who move in these oral, mnemonically tooled grooves," p. 35.

[8] Karl H. Bottcher, "The Narrative Technique in Achebe's Novels," *New African Literature and the Arts* 13/14 (1972), 7.

[9] Ong, pp. 45-46. See Bottcher on narrator's distance, pp. 1-5.

[10] Unpublished essay as quoted by Ron Scollon, "Rhythmic Integration of Ordinary Talk," in *Analyzing Discourse: Text and Talk*, ed. Deborah Tannen (Georgetown: Georgetown University Press, 1982) p. 337. See also Emmanuel Obeichina, *Culture, Tradition and Society in the West African Novel* (Cambridge: Cambridge University Press, 1975), p. 174.: "The main impulse in (Nigerian novelist Gabriel Okara's) *The Voice* obviously derives from the oral tradition . . . especially his deliberate repetitions, his metaphorical and hyperbolic elaborations and his colloquial rhythm."

[11] Quoted in Jahnheinz Jahn, *Muntu* (New York: Grove Press, 1961), pp. 164-166. See original, Senghor, "L'Esthétique Négro-Africaine," *Liberté I, Négritude el Humanisme* (Paris: Editions du Seuil, 1964), pp. 211-212; and his premise: "*Image* et *rhythme*, ce sont les deux traits fondamentaux du style négro-africain," p. 209. See also Obeichina: "The most striking feature of Okara's art is the repetition of single words, phrases, sentences, images for symbols, a feature highly developed in traditional narrative," p. 173; and Daniel P. Biebuyck, *Hero and Chief, Epic Literature from the Banyanga (Zaire Republic)* (Berkeley: University of California Press, 1978), p. 79: "Somewhat related to the formulaic system are the innumerable repetitions that add emphasis, effect, clarity and thus give fullness to the description [and] lend sonority, additional rhythm, and emphasis to the statements."

[12] Ibid., p. 168.

[13] Robert Kellogg, "Literature, Nonliterature, and Oral Tradition," *New Literary History* 5 (Spring 1977), 532. This issue of *NLH* has a valuable collection of essays on "Oral Cultures and Oral Performances."

[14] Roger Fowler, *Linguistics and the Novel* (London: Methuen, 1977), p. 28: "the surface structure of a text (which is a sequence of sentences) has, like the surface structure of a sentence, qualities such as sequence, rhythm, spatial and temporal expressiveness." Raymond Chapman, *The Language of English Literature* (London: Edward Arnold, 1982), pp. 54-55: "We have seen that the

traditional metres of English poetry have some connection with the rhythms of ordinary speech. . . . Rhythm of course is not confined to poetry . . . prose can have its distinctive cadence." Richard Ohmann, "Generative Grammars and the Concept of Literary Style," in *Linguistics and Literary Style*, ed. Donald Freeman (New York: Hold, Rinehart and Winston, 1970; previously published 1964), p. 260: "let me state this dogmatically—in prose, at least, rhythm as perceived is largely dependent upon syntax, and even upon content, not upon stress, intonation, and juncture alone."

[15] Fowler, pp. 60, 63. See also Michael Riffaterre, "Criteria for Style Analysis," in *Essays on the Language of Literature*, eds. Seymour Chapman and Samuel Levin (Boston: Houghton Mifflin, 1967), pp. 428-429.

[16] Raymond Chapman, p. 43: "One of the most common metrical lines in English poetry is the iambic pentameter. . . . It follows very closely the pattern of everyday speech. . . . The iambic pentameter can be given many variations, but it remains close to what sounds 'natural' in English."

[17] David Carroll, *Chinua Achebe* (New York: Twayne, 1970), pp. 37, 47.

[18] Solomon O. Iyasere, "Narrative Techniques in 'Things Fall Apart,'" *New Letters* 40, 3 (1974), 76. See also Iyasere, "Oral Tradition in the Criticism of African Literature," *Journal of Modern African Studies* 13, 1 (1975), 111-114.

[19] Robert Wren, *Achebe's World* (Washington, D.C.: Three Continents Press, 1980), pp. 23 ff.

[20] Bottcher, pp. 1-12.

[21] Cf. John, p. 165; and J. H. Kwabena Nketia, *The Music of Africa* (New York: Norton, 1974), p. 136: "the crucial point in polyrhythmic procedures . . . is the spacing or the placement of rhythmic patterns that are related to one another at different points in time so as to produce the anticipated integrated structure." All of Chapter 12 is relevant here. Isadore Okepewho, *The Epic in Africa: Toward a Poetic of Oral Performance* (New York: Columbia University Press, 1979), pp. 61-62, asks, "What is the nature of this musical element in African heroic song?" and responds, "one fundamental aspect, its polyrhythmic nature, is relevant here. . . . Polyrhythms . . . vary as one moves from east to west, with West Africa as the region of greatest complexity."

[22] Bottcher, p. 7.

[23] For discussion of the feminine, see Ernest Champion, "The Story of a Man and His People," *NALF* 6 (9172), 274; G. D. Killam, *The Novels of Chinua Achebe* (New York: Africana, 1969), pp. 20 ff.; Iyasere, "Narrative. . . ," pp. 79 ff.; Wilfred Cartey, *Whispers from a Continent* (New York: Random House, 1969), Chapter 1, "Mother and Child." Awareness of the masculine/feminine element is now widely manifested by critics.

[24] Wren, p. 23.

[25] Ibid., p. 24.

[26] *Myth, Literature, and the African World* (Cambridge: Cambridge University Press, 1976), pp. 144-145.

[27] Cartey, p. 100.

[28] Arthur Ravenscroft, *Chinua Achebe* (London: Longmans, Green, 1969), p. 13.

[29] Cf. Senghor, p. 214: "Il y a plus, la structure de la phrase négro-africaine est naturellement rythmée. Car, tandis que les langues indo-européennes usent d'une syntaxe logique de subordination, les langues négro-

africaines recourent, plus volontirs, à une syntaxe intuitive de *coordination et de juxtaposition*." See also Robert Kauffman, "African Rhythm: A Reassessment," *Ethnomusicology* 24, 3 (1980), 402, 406.

[30] In the quotation from p. 123 the repetition of "he" and active verbs— "He knew," "he would do," "he would rebuild."—confirms our sense that Okonkwo is operating outside the cultural rhythms of the clan. Marjorie Winters in "An Objective Approach to Achebe's Style," *Research in African Literatures* 32, 1 (1981), 55-68, describes the length of the narrator's sentences, his spare use of adjectives and adverbs, the "unusual number of "introductory demonstratives," the clarity achieved by his "redundancy of connective signposts" ('and so') "as well as other repetitious elements." Her approach differs from mine but her results do not oppose conclusions drawn here.

[31] Lloyd Brown, "Cultural Norms and Modes of Perception in Achebe's Fiction," *Critical Perspectives on Nigerian Literature*, ed. Bernth Lindfors (Washington, D.C.: Three Continents Press, 1976) p. 133.

[32] Chinua Achebe, "Language and the Destiny of Man," *Morning Yet on Creation Day* (New York: Doubleday, 1975), pp. 56-57.

[33] Achebe, "The African Writer and the English Language," *Morning Yet on Creation Day*, pp. 101-102.

[34] Achebe, "Where Angels Fear to Tread," *Morning Yet on Creation Day*, p. 79.

Narrative Techniques in *Things Fall Apart*

Solomon O. Iyasere

No West African fiction in English has received as much critical attention as *Things Fall Apart*, Chinua Achebe's first and most impressive novel. In defending its importance, most critics link its value solely to its theme, which they take to be the disintegration of an almost Edenic traditional society as a result of its contact and conflict with Western practices and beliefs. These enthusiastic critics, such as Gleason and Killam, are primarily interested in the socio-cultural features of the work, and stress the historical picture of a traditional Ibo village community without observing how this picture is delimited, how this material serves the end of art. This approach, which cannot withstand critical scrutiny, does great violence to the text and denies it the artistic vitality they so vigorously claim for it.

Overemphasizing the ways in which Okonkwo represents certain values fundamental to the Umuofia society, Killam turns Okonkwo into an embodiment of the values of this society, averring, "Okonkwo was one of the greatest men of his time, the embodiment of Ibo values, the man who better than most symbolizes his race" (*The Novels of Chinua Achebe*, p. 17). Eustace Palmer, a moralistic critic, presents a similar interpretation but extends Okonkwo's role from champion to victim:

> Okonkwo is what his society has made him, for his most conspicuous qualities are a response to the demands of his society. If he is plagued by fear of failure and of weakness it is because his society put such a premium on success. . . . Okonkwo is a personification of his society's values, and he is determined to succeed in this rat-race. (*An Introduction to the African Novel*, p. 53)

The inaccuracies of this view derive from disregarding the particularities of the rhetoric of Achebe's controlled presentation.   Killam and Palmer take as authoritative Okonkwo's vision of himself as a great leader and savior of Umuofia and so fail to realize that this vision is based on a limited perception of the values of that society.   Nowhere in the novel is Okonkwo presented as either the embodiment or the victim of Umuofia's traditional laws and customs.   To urge that he is either, as do Killam and Palmer, is to reduce the work to a sentimental melodrama, rob Okonkwo of his tragic stature, and deny the reader's sympathy for him.

More responsive to the novel's simultaneous sympathy for and critical judgment of Okonkwo, David Carroll observes:

> As Okonkwo's life moves quickly to its tragic end, one is reminded forcibly of another impressive but wrongheaded hero, Henchard in *The Mayor of Caster-bridge*. They share in obsessive need for success and status, they subordinate all their private relations to this end, and both have an inability to understand the tolerant, skeptical societies in which their novel single-mindedness succeeds. . . . Viewed in the perspective of the Wessex, rustic way of life, Henchard is crass, brutal, and dangerous; but when this way of life as a whole is threatened with imminent destruction, then his fierce resistance takes on a certain grandeur. The reader's sympathy describes a similar trajectory as it follows Okonkwo's career. By the values of Umuofia his inadequacies are very apparent; but when the alien religion begins to question and undermine these values, Okonkwo, untroubled by the heart-searching of the community, springs to its defense and acts.
>
> (*Chinua Achebe*, pp. 62-63)

Carroll's comment is to the point in directing our attention to the crucial limitations Okonkwo places on his relationship to and acceptance of Umuofia's standards.   But simply focusing attention on this matter is not sufficient; we must see how Achebe is able to achieve this control of sympathy for Okonkwo.

Things Fall Apart seems a simple novel, but it is deceptively so.   On closer inspection, we see that it is provocatively complex, interweaving significant themes: love, compassion, colonialism, achievement, honor, and individualism.   In treating these themes, Achebe employs a variety of devices, such as proverbs, folktales, rituals, and the juxtaposition of characters and episodes to provide a double view of the Ibo society of Umuofia and the central character, Okonkwo. The traditional Ibo society that emerges is a complex one: ritualistic and rigid yet in many ways surprisingly flexible. In this society, a child is valued more than any material acquisition, yet the innocent, loving child, Ikemefuna, is denied love, denied life, by the rigid tribal laws and customs. Outwardly, Umuofia is a world of serenity, harmony, and communal activities but inwardly it is torn by the individual's personal doubts and fears. It is also a society in which "age was respected . . . but achievement was revered." It is this sustained view of the duality of the traditional Ibo society that the novel consistently presents in order to create and intensify the sense of tragedy and make the reader understand the dilemma that shapes and destroys the life of Okonkwo.

No episode reveals more dramatically the concomitant rigidity and flexibility of the society than the trial scene in which the domestic conflict between Uzowulu and his wife Mgbafo is settled. Uzowulu has beaten his wife so often and so severely that at last she has fled to her family for protection from him. While such conflicts are usually settled on a personal level, Uzowulu is the kind of man who will listen only to the judgment of the great *egwugwu*, the masked ancestor spirits of the clan. This ceremony proceeds with marked ritual (*TFA*, p. 85).

The ritualistic procedure of this event reflects the seriousness and formality with which the people of Umuofia deal with internal problems, even trivial ones, that undermine or threaten the peaceful coexistence of the clans. The stereotyped incantatory exchange of greeting, the ceremonious way in which the spirits appear, the ritual greeting, "Uzowulu's body, I salute you," and Uzowulu's response, "Our father, my hand has touched the ground," even the gestures of these masked spirits, define the formality of the society and dramatize the fact that the peace of the tribe as a whole takes precedence over personal considerations. The decrees of the gods are always carried out with dispatch, even if it means a ruthless violation of human impulses, as in the murder of Ikemefuna or the throwing away of twins. But this formality does not preclude dialogue, probing and debate, aptly demonstrated in that the parties involved in the conflict are allowed to present their opposing, even hostile views. The way this domestic issue is resolved reveals the unqualified emphasis the people of Umuofia place on harmony and peaceful coexistence (*TFA*, p. 89).

The formality of this event, the firmness with which the society controls impending disorder, becomes even more apparent when contrasted with the spontaneous communal feasting that precedes it—the coming of the locust. This sudden occurrence aptly demonstrates the joy and vitality of the society when it is not beleaguered by internal disharmony (*TFA*, pp. 54-55).

The overabundance of locusts provides an equal measure of joy for Umuofia. While the people restrain themselves enough to heed the elders' instruction on how to catch the insects this control of happiness is momentary, and no one spares either time or effort in responding to this unexpected feast. For the moment, Umuofia is at peace; Okonkwo and his sons are united in sharing the joy which envelopes the community. Against the joyfully harmonic rhythm of this event, the withdrawn, controlled formalism of the judgment of the *egwugwu* stands in sharp relief. By juxtaposing these events, Achebe orchestrates the modulating rhythms of Umuofia, the alternating patterns of spontaneous joy and solemn justice. This modulation of rhythms developed out of the juxtaposition of contrasting events operates also within the framework of the same episode. The suddenness with which the locusts descend on the people, bringing joy, is matched by the suddenness with which that joy is taken away. The very moment that Okonkwo and his sons sit feasting, Ezeudu enters to tell Okonkwo of the decree of the Oracle of the Hills and Caves (*TFA*, pp. 55-56).

Just as Okonkwo's response to the celebration of feasting is controlled by the almost simultaneous announcement of the doom of the innocent child, Ikemefuna, so the narrator modulates the reader's response to the contrasting values and customs of Umuofia. On the very day Ikemefuna sits happily with his "father," Ezeudu somberly states, "Yes, Umuofia has decided to kill him."

Similarly, in order to articulate and call attention to the rigidity of the Ibo code of values in requiring the exile of Okonkwo for the inadvertent killing of Ezeudu's son, Achebe skillfully orchestrates the circumstances of the boy's death. In presenting this scene, Achebe emphasizes the atmosphere, the action, and the situation without individualizing Okonkwo's role. Such deliberate attention to the circumstances that day intensifies the sense of accidental occurrence. The death of Ezeudu's son comes as a result of the situation, of the circumstances, not as any deliberate act on Okonkwo's part. With this sense of chance established, the scene makes more apparent the rigidity of the tribal laws in dealing with this accidental event:

> The only course open for Okonkwo was to flee from the clan. It was a crime against the earth goddess to kill a clansman, and a man who committed it must flee from the land. The crime was of two kinds, male and female. Okonkwo had committed the female because it had been inadvertent. He could return to the clan after seven years.   (*TFA*, p. 117)

In probing and evaluating this code whose rigidity negates circumstantial and human considerations, the thoughtful Obierika questions, "Why should a man suffer so grievously for an offense he had committed inadvertently?"

Obierika's thoughts reflect the submerged fears of the village elders, particularly Uchendu, Okonkwo's uncle, and Ezeudu, as well as the doubts and questions of Okonkwo's wives and even his son Nwoye. Indeed, he gives voice to the very question the reader himself asks.

The inflexibility of this tribal code and its application is revealed not only in the formal decrees of the Oracles and the judgments of the *egwugwu* but also in the small details of every day life. The simple act of a cow getting loose in the fields is met with a harsh penalty (*TFA*, pp. 108-109). Since the preservation of crops is essential in an agricultural society, the imposition of a severe fine on those whose animals destroy the produce is understandable. But the crucial point the narrator stresses here is that the laws are applied with absolute rigidity, with no regard for mitigating circumstances. Even though the responsible party in this instance was only a small child being watched by his father, who does not usually watch the children, while the mother was busy helping another prepare a feast to ensure the proper observance of the marriage ceremonies, the same penalty is exacted. Just as Okonkwo is harshly punished for an inadvertent act which occurred while he was observing the proper funeral rites of the clan, so is Ezelagbo's husband punished for an offense his small child committed both unintentionally and unknowingly. In these small ways, Achebe succeeds in presenting the inflexibility of the code of values of Umuofia as it responds to any threat, no matter how small, to the overall stability of the clan.

Yet to insist that this code is entirely inflexible is to present only one-half of the picture. The people of Umuofia can

adapt their code to accommodate the less successful, even effeminate men, like Okonkwo's father, Unoka, despite the fact that
according to their standards of excellence, solid personal
achievement and manly stature are given unqualified emphasis.
This adaptability to changing or different situations is further
demonstrated in Ogbuefi Ezeudu's comment on the punishment meted out to Okonkwo for his violation of the sacred
Week of Peace.

> 'It has not always been so,' he said. 'My father
> told me that he had been told that in the past a man
> who broke the peace was dragged on the ground
> through the village until he died. But after a while
> this custom was stopped because it spoiled the peace
> which it was meant to preserve.'
>
> 'Somebody told me yesterday,' said one of the
> younger men, 'that in some clans it is an abomination for
> a man to die during the Week of Peace.'
>
> 'It is indeed true,' said Ogbuefi Ezeudu. 'They have
> that custom in Obadoani. If a man dies at this time he
> is not buried but cast into the Evil Forest. It is a bad cus-
> tom which these people observe because they lack un-
> derstanding. They throw away large numbers of men
> and women without burial. And what is the result?
> Their clan is full of evil spirits of these unburied dead,
> hungry to do harm to the living.'   (TFA, p. 33)

It seems clear from this instance that in some ways the social
code of Umuofia is responsive to change; if the people find elements of the code contradictory, they will alter them, provided
such modification does not conflict with the will of the gods.
This receptivity to change is coupled with a willingness to accept
and accommodate even those who do not perfectly conform to
their ways, in accordance with the proverbial wisdom, "Let the
kite perch and let the eagle perch too. If one says no to the other,
let his wing break" (TFA, pp. 21-22). Though Unoka was the
subject of jest, he was not cast out, and even the albinos, whom
the Ibos of Umuofia consider aliens, were accepted members of
the clan, for, as Uchendu indicates to Obierika, "'There is no
story that is not true,' said Uchendu. 'The world has no end,
and what is good among one people is an abomination with
others. We have albinos among us. Do you not think that they
came by mistake, that they have strayed from their way to a land
where everybody is like them?'" (TFA, p. 130). Throughout the
novel, this complex, dualistic nature of the customs and traditions of the Ibo society of Umuofia is made clear. This duality is

well presented through Achebe's technique of skillfully juxta-posing contrasting events, events which define and articulate the code of values of the tradition oriented people. On the one hand, we see the villagers actively engaged in a spontaneous communal activity, such as enjoying a marriage feast, or gather-ing and sharing the locusts, while, on the other hand, we see the rigid application of tribal laws and decrees of the gods which often deny and violate human responses.

These elements are set in opposition to one another to give a complete, if self-contradictory, view of the society. To ac-cept and emphasize only one aspect is to oversimplify and de-fend, as does Okonkwo, a limited perception. It is against this balanced view of the proud traditional Ibo society that the novel invites us to evaluate the actions and tragic life of the central character, Okonkwo. Only through such examination do the problems of Okonkwo's relationship to the culture of his people become clear.

As a careful reading of *Things Fall Apart* reveals, one of Achebe's great achievements is his ability to keep alive our sym-pathy for Okonkwo despite our moral revulsion from some of his violent, inhuman acts. With Obierika, we condemn him for participating in the killing of the innocent boy, Ikemefuna. We despise him for denying his son, Nwoye, love, understanding, and compassion. And we join the village elders in disapproving Okonkwo's uncompromisingly rigid attitude toward unsuccess-ful, effeminate men such as his father, Unoka, or Usugo. Yet we share with the narrator a sustained sympathy for him. We do not simply identify with him, nor defend his actions, nor admire him as an heroic individual. We do give him our innermost sympathies because we know from his reactions to his own vio-lence that deep within him he is not a cruel man. It is this con-trasting, dualistic view of Okonkwo that the narrator consis-tently presents. On the one hand, we see Okonkwo participating in the brutal killing of Ikemefuna, his "son," but on the other, we see him brooding over this violent deed for three full days. In another instance, we see him dispassionately castigating his fragile, loving daughter, Ezinma, and deeply regretting that she is not a boy, while on another occasion we see him struggling all night to save her from *iba* or returning again and again to the cave to protect her from harm at the hands of Chielo, priestess of *Agbala*.

Throughout the novel, Okonkwo is presented as a man whose life is ruled by one overriding passion: to become success-ful, powerful, rich, found a dynasty, and become one of the lords of the clan of Umuofia. And Okonkwo's unflagging commit-ment is not without cause, for

> . . . his whole life was dominated by fear, the fear of failure and of weakness. It was deeper and more inti-mate than the fear of evil and capricious gods and of magic, the fear of the forest and of the forces of nature, malevolent, red in tooth and claw. Okonkwo's fear was greater than these. It was not external but lay deep within himself. It was the fear of himself, lest he should be found to resemble his father. And so Okonkwo was ruled by one passion—to hate everything that his father Unoka had loved. One of those things was gentleness and another was idleness.
>
> (*TFA*, pp. 16-17)

Emphasis here is placed on Okonkwo's divided self, especially on his inner struggle to control and suppress his fears of failure which arise in reaction to his father's disastrous life and shame-ful death. In some respects, the reader's initial reaction is to identify with Okonkwo, to join with him in severe condemna-tion of his father, for "Unoka the grown up was a failure. He was poor and his wife and children had barely enough to eat. People laughed at him because he was a loafer, and they swore never to lend him any more money because he never paid back" (*TFA*, p. 9). In modulating this initial response, the narrator also makes it quite clear that among these same people, "a man was judged according to his worth and not according to the worth of his father," and that while achievement was revered, age was re-spected. In violently repudiating all that his father represented, Okonkwo repudiates not only his undignified irresponsibility, but also those positive qualities of love and compassion and sen-sitivity (*TFA*, pp. 8, 10). Many of the qualities which to Okonkwo were marks of femininity and weakness are the same qualities which were respected by the society Okonkwo wished to champion. In a larger sense, Okonkwo's rigid repudiation of his father's "unmanliness" violates a necessary aspect of the soci-ety's code of values. We come to see that in suppressing his fears and those attributes which he considers a sign of weakness, Okonkwo denies as well those human responses of love and understanding which Umuofia recognizes as requisite for great-ness.

This obsession with proving and preserving his manliness dominates Okonkwo's entire life, both public and private: "He ruled his household with a heavy hand. His wives, especially the youngest, lived in perpetual fear of his fiery temper, and so did his little children" (*TFA*, p. 16). Even in the informal, relaxed story-telling sessions, Okonkwo sees a threat to himself and his "dynasty," for these stories will make women of his sons, make them like their grandfather rather than like their father. So, at those times, "Okonkwo encouraged the boys to sit with him in his *obi*, and he told them stories of the land—masculine stories of violence and bloodshed" (*TFA*, p. 52).

No episode in the novel dramatizes Okonkwo's desire to assert his manliness more clearly than the killing of Ikemefuna whom Okonkwo loves as his own.

It is the closeness of this father-son relationship, reiterated in the feasting on the locusts, that Ezeudu interrupts to tell Okonkwo that Ikemefuna must die. But Ezeudu provides more than this stark message; as a respected elder of the clan he also advises Okonkwo on his conduct in heeding the decree, "'Yes, Umuofia has decided to kill him. The Oracle of the Hills and Caves has pronounced it. They will take him outside Umuofia as is the custom, and kill him there. But I want you to have nothing to do with it. He calls you his father.'" Though his feeling for the boy comes through in his effort to cloak the grim reality from the youth's eyes—"later in the day he called Ikemefuna and told him that he was to be taken home the next day" (*TFA*, p. 56)—Okonkwo nevertheless disregards Ezeudu's advice and accompanies the men in their brutal task—"Okonkwo got ready quickly and the part set out with Ikemefuna carrying the pot of wine" (*TFA*, pp. 56-57). This same mixture of feelings controls Okonkwo's actions on that mission. He walks behind the others and gradually draws to the rear as the moment of execution arrives; indeed, he looks away when one of the men raises his machete to strike the boy. But he is forced by his own dogged insistence on masculinity to deal the fatal blow. The child runs to Okonkwo for protection but finds instead the cold, hard steel of Okonkwo's machete: "As the man who had cleared his throat drew up and raised his machete, Okonkwo looked away. He heard the blow. The pot fell and broke in the sand. He heard Ikemefuna cry, 'My father, they have killed me!' as he ran towards him. Dazed with fear, Okonkwo drew his machete and cut him down" (*TFA*, p. 59). He does so, as the narrator affirms,

because "he was afraid of being thought weak." So extreme is his
desire that he might not appear weak, that he might not be like
his father, that Okonkwo blinds himself to the wisdom of the
advice of the elder Ezeudu, the wisdom Obierika reasserts, "'If I
were you I would have stayed at home . . . if the Oracle said that
my son should be killed I would neither dispute it nor be the
one to do it'" (*TFA*, pp. 64-65). So determined is his effort to be
known for achievement, which his society reveres, that
Okonkwo gives no heed to the wisdom of age, which his society
respects. The way which both Ezeudu and Obierika espouse is
the way of compromise, of blending the masculine and feminine, but this is a compromise of which Okonkwo is incapable.

For the most part, Okonkwo resorts to violence in order to
maintain control of a situation and assert his manliness. Even
in his relationship to his *chi*, or personal god, Okonkwo exerts
force to mold his *chi* to his will. But in wrestling with his *chi*, in
coercing it into submission to his will, Okonkwo violates the
conventional, harmonious relationship one has with his personal god: "The Ibo people have a proverb that when a man says
yes, his *chi* says yes also. Okonkwo said yes very strongly, so his
chi agreed. And not only his *chi*, his clan, too" (TFA, p. 29). On
all levels, then, Okonkwo must dominate and control events; by
sheer force and, if necessary, brutality, Okonkwo bends to his
will his *chi*, his family, and his clan. If "things fall apart," it is
because "the center cannot hold"—because Okonkwo cannot
maintain the precarious tension which forcefully holds in place
chi, family, and clan.

Yet Okonkwo is not wholly a brute force. Even at the very
moment of his violence against Ikemefuna we glimpse the humanity locked inside: "As the man who had cleared his throat
drew up and raised his machete, Okonkwo looked away."
Okonkwo looks away not because he is a coward, nor because,
like his father, he could not stand the sight of blood; after all, "in
Umuofia's latest war he was the first to bring home a human
head," (*TFA*, p. 14), his fifth. Okonkwo looks away because this
brutal act is too much even for his eyes and his "buried humanity" struggles to express itself.

The narrator includes these subtle details which emphasize the submerged human responses of Okonkwo to explore
Okonkwo's tragic dilemma and modulate our responses to him.
Re-emphasizing these positive human aspects which Okonkwo
possesses but which he struggles to stifle lest he appear weak, the

narrator sympathetically relates Okonkwo's reaction to his own violence, without approving the violent act itself:

> Okonkwo did not taste any food for two days after the death of Ikemefuna. He drank palm-wine from morning till night, and his eyes were red and fierce like the eyes of a rat when it was caught by the tail and dashed against the floor.
>
> He did not sleep at night. He tried not to think about Ikemefuna, but the more he tried the more he thought about him. Once he got up from his bed and walked about his compound. But he was so weak that his legs could scarcely carry him. He felt like a drunken giant walking with the limbs of a mosquito. Now and then a cold shiver descended on his head and spread down his body.

In private, unguarded moments like this, Okonkwo cannot but allow his "buried humanity" to express itself. But he does not allow his reaction to Ikemefuna's death to lead to self-pity and, in so doing, does not allow our sympathy for him to degenerate into pity. In his rigid view, any brooding, introspection, or questioning is a sign of weakness: "Okonkwo was not a man of thought but of action" (*TFA*, p. 66). For this reason, on the morning of the third day of brooding over Ikemefuna, Okonkwo calls for food and answers his brooding with action. His attitude these three days cause him to question himself, but these questions do not investigate motive nor justify his deed; instead, they chastise him for his weakness in responding so to the death of his "son." "He sprang to his feet, hung his goatskin bag on his shoulder and went to visit his friend, Obierika" (*TFA*, p. 63). It is now daytime and no one must see Okonkwo submit to the human feeling of grief.

Publicly, especially among the members of his own clan, Okonkwo struggles to maintain the image of an unusually calm and stalwart individual, a man worthy to be a lord of the clan. It is only in private—and often in the dark—that Okonkwo spontaneously reveals the love and warmth he feels for his family. In the dark, he rushes to protect his daughter from harm by Chielo; without thought, he rushes to save her from *iba*. Ironically, it is with the same quickness that Okonkwo prepared for the killing of Ikemefuna that he attends to the dying Ezinma (*TFA*, pp. 72-73).

For Okonkwo, the conflict between private self and public man is the conflict between the feminine and masculine princi-

ples. His inability to comprehend the fact that those feminine attributes he vigorously suppresses in himself are necessary for
greatness is revealed in his näive comments on the deaths of
Ogbuefi Ndulue and his eldest wife, Ozoemena (*TFA*, pp. 65-66).

The sudden, willed death of Ozoemena is strange, as
Ofoedu, Obierika, and Okonkwo agree. Yet, as is characteristic of
Okonkwo, he can perceive and respond only to the obvious and
well-defined. What Okonkwo cannot understand in this
episode, despite Obierika's explanation, is the full significance of
Ozoemena's death, especially as it is a willed response to her
husband's death. The union in life and in death of Ndulue and
Ozoemena is a symbolic dramatization of the union of the masculine and feminine attributes essential in a great man. Ndulue
was a great warrior and a great man, the respected elder of his
village, because he was able to find that balance of strength and
sensitivity, of masculine and feminine principles. And it is this
union men such as Ndulue and Ezeudu are able to achieve and
which Umuofia respects and seeks in its leaders. For Okonkwo,
one is either a man or a woman; there can be no compromise,
no composite. He is baffled by Ndulue's relationship to Ozoemena, for to him a strong man would in no way depend on a
woman. This one-sided concept of what it takes to be a man determines Okonkwo's actions and attitudes, and can be seen
clearly in his thoughts about his children. To him, Ezinma
should have been a boy and Nwoye has "too much of his
mother in him" (*TFA*, p. 64).

Okonkwo has held this monochromatic view of what
people should be, with men and women performing sexually-
defined tasks and exhibiting equally well-defined characteristics,
since his youth. Traumatized by his father's failure as owing to
his gentleness and idleness, Okonkwo determines to be all that
his father was not—firm and active. But in living up to this design, Okonkwo becomes inflexible and his action allows no
room for reflection. Throughout his life he clings to this pattern
steadfastly and without question. Such a rigid commitment to a
code of behavior and design for action thwarts Okonkwo's personal development. He does not grow and change with age and
experience; as a man he is dedicated to the same stereotypes he
formed in his youth. Even after his code fails him and necessi-
tates his exile, Okonkwo cannot see the limitations of that code
in its denial of the "feminine" principles. While in exile in his
mother's land, Mbanta, Okonkwo is lectured on the importance

of these feminine principles by the elder Uchendu, but still Okonkwo cannot see:

> 'Can you tell me, Okonkwo, why it is that one of the commonest names we give our children is Nneka, or 'Mother is Supreme'? We all know that a man is the head of the family and his wives do his bidding. A child belongs to its father and his family and not to its mother and her family. A man belongs to his father-land and not to his motherland. And yet we say Nneka—'Mother is Supreme.' Why is that?'
> There was silence. 'I want Okonkwo to answer me,' said Uchendu.
> 'I do not know the answer,' Okonkwo replied.

Through probing questions, Uchendu deliberately attempts to lead Okonkwo to an understanding of the importance of the feminine qualities which Okonkwo seeks to deny: he reminds Okonkwo that the consequence of this denial, which has already resulted in Okonkwo's alienation from his clan, his family, and himself, is doom. But Okonkwo is not the type of man who does things half way, "not even for fear of a goddess." He is too "manly," too single-minded to deal with subtleties which do not fit easily into his well-defined code of action. For this reason, he cannot respond to Uchendu's questions, for they directly threaten his rigid philosophy of life.

Uchendu, like Ndulue and Ezeudu, represents the traditional way of life which allows for flexibility and compromise within its exacting system. And in rejecting compromise and flexibility, Okonkwo rejects the values of the society he determines to champion. In contrasting these two antithetical modes of perception and patterns of action, the narrator illustrates the extent to which Okonkwo has alienated himself from his society. The contrasting modes of action determine the different reactions of Uchendu and Okonkwo to Obierika's tales of the killing of the white man on the iron horse, in Abame, which in turn led to the death of a large number of villagers. Hearing this tale of disaster and death, Uchendu ground his teeth together audibly and then burst out, "Never kill a man who says nothing. Those men of Abame were fools. What did they know about the man?" (*TFA*, p. 129). As is characteristic of a wise and prudent man, Uchendu blames the people of Abame for not being cautious and for fighting a "war of blame" which the society condemns. But Okonkwo sees the whole situation as supporting his method of turning to violence for a solution to all problems. Instead of questioning and seeking a compromise between conflicting views, Okonkwo demands a violent action, "'They were fools,' said Okonkwo after a pause. 'They had been warned that danger was ahead. The should have armed themselves with their guns and their machetes even when they went to the market'" (*TFA*, p. 130).

Throughout his life, then, Okonkwo is bound to violence. He rigidly commits himself to a code of values which negates human response and severs himself from his traditional roots. Even at crucial moments when all indications point to the limitation and inadequacy of his rigid system, Okonkwo still holds firmly to these values, even to his death. The failure of his code is clear in his attitude toward Nwoye and in his son's subsequent rejection of him. The feelings of tenderness and affection Okonkwo has so long suppressed erupt as violence. When he is confronted by the limitation of his values in responding to human needs, especially manifest in Nwoye's turning to Christianity for an answer to these needs, Okonkwo's recourse to violence is even more extreme:

> It was late afternoon before Nwoye returned. He went into the *obi* and saluted his father, but he did not answer. Nwoye turned round to walk into the inner compound when his father, suddenly overcome with fury, sprang to his feet and gripped him by the neck.
> 'Where have you been?' he stammered.
> Nwoye struggled to free himself from the choking grip.
> 'Answer me,' roared Okonkwo, 'before I kill you!' He seized a heavy stick that lay on the dwarf wall and hit him two or three savage blows.
> 'Answer me!' he roared again. Nwoye stood looking at him and did not say a word. The women were screaming outside, afraid to go in.
> 'Leave that boy at once!' said a voice in the outer compound.
> It was Okonkwo's uncle, Uchendu. 'Are you mad?'
> Okonkwo did not answer. But he left hold of Nwoye, who walked away and never returned.
> (*TFA*, p. 141)

The bondage in which Okonkwo has kept his "feminine" qualities is the bondage in which he has tried to keep Nwoye. Coercing, cajoling, threatening, and even beating his son into conforming to his ways, Okonkwo alienates the "dynasty" his actions sought to insure. For Nwoye will not be kept enslaved to

Okonkwo's ways; he seeks release from bondage in the new religion of the white man.

Okonkwo's tragedy is not merely that he fails to understand the needs of his son Nwoye but that he also cannot comprehend certain of the society's values. Unable to change himself, he will not accept change in others, in the world around him, in the people of Umuofia. When he returns from exile, Okonkwo faces an altered society, a society that in its flexibility has allowed a place for the white Christian missionaries. Like the recalcitrant Rev. Smith, Okonkwo views the situation in terms of absolute, irreconcilable antipodes.

When the entire clan gathers to decide how to deal with the inroads established by the missionaries, Okonkwo's response is predictable. He will brook no compromise and demands a violent repulsion of the new religion. But this recourse to violence is not the view of this society any more now than it was in the past. Indeed, Okonkwo's views set him apart from his clan at this moment as earlier in his exile: but it is too late for Okonkwo to change now. If the society will not violently repel this threat, Okonkwo will. Compelled by his own uncompromising attitudes as they confront and clash with the equally adamant positions of Rev. Smith, Okonkwo turns to the only means he knows—violence—to solve the problem:

> In a flash Okonkwo drew his machete. The messenger crouched to avoid the blow. It was useless. Okonkwo's machete descended twice and the man's head lay beside his uniformed body.
>
> The waiting backcloth jumped into tumultuous life and the meeting was stopped. Okonkwo stood looking at the dead man. He knew that Umuofia would not go to war. He knew because they had let the other messengers escape. They had broken into tumult instead of action. He discerned fright in that tumult. He heard voices asking, 'Why did he do it?'
>
> He wiped his machete on the sand and went away.
>
> (*TFA*, pp. 187-188)

When the society does not respond as he does, Okonkwo comes to the sudden, belated realization that he is all alone, set apart from his clan by the values he holds. This most recent act of violence severs finally the precarious link between Okonkwo and his people. And, as before with the killing of Ikemefuna and the beating of Nwoye, Okonkwo's brutal force creates for him an even greater dilemma than the one he resorted to violence to solve. If at the edge of Umuofia before this last violent act, Okonkwo is now pushed outside his society. He cannot return. He cannot begin again. Having no place in this new Umuofia, driven out by his own inability to bend and change, Okonkwo ends his life as he lived it—by violence.

This act of violence against himself ironically fulfills Obierika's "request" of several years ago:

> 'I do not know how to thank you.'
> 'I can tell you,' said Obierika. 'Kill one of your sons for me.'
> 'That will not be enough,' said Okonkwo.
> 'Then kill yourself,' said Obierika.
> 'Forgive me,' said Okonkwo, smiling. 'I shall not talk about thanking you any more.' (*TFA*, pp. 131-132)

Okonkwo's suicide is, as Obierika explains (*TFA*, pp. 190-191), and offense against the earth, an abomination. Okonkwo's clansmen cannot touch him, cannot bury him, cannot consider him one of their own. In death, as in life, Okonkwo's commitment to achievement through violence ostracizes him from the very society he sought so desperately to champion and honor.

On the other hand, we do not justify Okonkwo's killing of the messenger in an effort to save the doomed way of life of his beleaguered clan, a way of life whose subtle codes Okonkwo does not understand. Nor do we approve his unflagging commitment to his own code which does not provide for life. Yet we sympathize with him, even in his death, though perhaps not so emotionally as Obierika who, at this moment, loses all sense of objectivity. Temporarily blind to Okonkwo's limitations, Obierika seems to make Okonkwo the innocent victim of the brutal laws of the white missionaries. Prior to this dramatic confrontation with the white missionaries, the narrator has made it inevitable that Okonkwo's violent actions will lead him to his doom. At the same time, this knowledge does not deny him our innermost sympathies, especially when we evaluate his actions as juxtaposed against the actions of the "purist," Rev. Smith, who "saw things as back and white. And black was evil. He saw the world as a battlefield in which the children of light were locked in mortal combat with the sons of darkness. He spoke in his sermons about sheep and goats and about wheat and tares. He believed in slaying the prophet of Baal" (*TFA*, p. 169). Rev. Smith's approach was, in all respects, antithetical to that of his predecessor, Rev. Brown, and Achebe shows Rev. Smith to be a far more vicious, brutal, and violent man than Okonkwo.

> There was a saying in Umuofia that as a man danced so the drums were beaten for him. Mr. Smith danced a furious step and so the drums went mad. The over-zealous converts who had smarted under Mr. Brown's restraining hand now flourished in full favor.

Following Rev. Smith's cue, an over-zealous convert, Enoch, likewise resorts to extreme actions, and goes so far as to unmask an *egwugwu*, throwing Umuofia into confusion (*TFA*, p. 170). In retaliation, the *egwugwu* swarm into the church and level it: "Mr. Smith stood his ground. But he could not save his church. When the *egwugwu* went away the red-earth church which Mr. Brown had built was a pile of ashes. And for the moment the spirit of the clan was satisfied" (*TFA*, p. 175). Replacing Rev. Brown's law of peace and love with his own code of aggression and hatred, Rev. Smith undoes the good Rev. Brown had accomplished. Rather than convert the heathen ways to Christian purpose, Rev. Smith determines to destroy the traditional practices. He will force the villagers to accept his ways and humiliate or eliminate those who don't.

Working through the District Commissioner, the new law of the land, Rev. Smith has the *egwugwu*, including Okonkwo, disgraced and humiliated, their heads shaved in testimony to their dishonor. Rev. Smith's malice goes far beyond Okonkwo's rigidity in ruthlessly dishonoring the customs of the Umuofia people and instigating an unprovoked attack on their religion. We are invited to condemn Rev. Smith's ruthless methods in converting these supposed heathens to his religion. Because we see Rev. Smith in such a negative light, we almost come to see his religion in the same terms. For these reasons, we sympathize with Okonkwo while we see the pointlessness of his violent action in killing the messenger and taking his own life.

Though Rev. Smith's actions tend to obfuscate the positive aspects of Christianity, we can still recall its essentially valuable tenets as lived and spread by Rev. Brown. This religion, with its emphasis on individual salvation and love responded to a need deeply felt by certain people in Umuofia, such as Obierika and Nwoye, but never openly expressed. Christianity answered these private fears and doubts over the arbitrariness of the gods' decrees, decrees which deny personal or human considerations in their application. Christianity is then the catalyst but not the primary cause of things falling apart. Umuofia was already disintegrating and re-forming, for Christianity would not have spread if it did not fill a pre-existing need. This new religion takes root and flourishes in the very place where the twins were thrown away and Ikemefuna was killed, the Evil Forest outside Umuofia.

From Achebe's juxtaposition of conflicting values and actions emerge the paradoxes and ironies of *Things Fall Apart*. The flexibility of Umuofia allows room for Christianity which in turn contributes to the passing of the traditional ways in fulfilling the needs the inflexibility of Umuofia left unanswered. For a time the traditional and the Christian can exist side by side in peace, before the coming of Rev. Smith and the return from exile of Okonkwo. Each man believes himself to be the champion of his society's religion and those customs so that ultimately—and paradoxically—he negates the very values he seeks to defend. This technique of juxtaposition works well in articulating the complexities and contradictions of Umuofia, of Okonkwo, and of the dilemma which arises when they confront Christianity.

The Sphinx and the Rough Beast: Linguistic Struggle in Chinua Achebe's *Things Fall Apart*

Julian N. Wasserman

As an African novel written in English yet relying on the author's extensive use of Ibo terminology and vocabulary, Chinua Achebe's *Things Fall Apart*[1] forcefully draws its readers' attention to the problematical relationship between language and cultural identity, for language is the arena in which the cultural struggle between the folkways of the Ibo of Nigeria and the "High Culture" of their British colonizers is ultimately fought.[2] Indeed, in his non-fiction, expository writings, Achebe has been quick to note the interdependency of language and culture, going so far as to argue that one cannot exist without the presence of the other.[3] Moreover, following well established linguistic theory, Achebe presents language as a force for shaping as well as expressing consciousness. In short, each language is a philosophy, so that any clash of philosophies must ultimately evolve into a conflict of language and symbol. The battle for men's minds is, then, foremost a battle for their tongues, and when one philosophy supersedes another, the victor must inevitably impose not only its precepts but the means of their formulation and transmission upon the vanquished.

From the very outset, the cultural conflict between the Ibo and the British missionaries is presented as a clash between two societies whose linguistic perspectives and identities are antithetical. The focal point of the rumors generated by the first appearance of the white man in Umuofia is the manner and content of the white men's speech (p. 129). When the presence of the white men becomes an established fact, the difference in language is offered by Obierika, one of the clan's elders, as the reason for the white man's violation of Ibo custom. When asked if the white man understands the customs of the Ibo, Obierika replies. "How can he when he does not even speak our tongue?" (p. 162).

Moreover, the linguistic tension around which the novel is consciously constructed is witnessed by the fact that the tale both begins and ends with the polar attitudes of the Ibo and the English in regard to the use of language. The novel virtually opens with a statement of Ibo linguistic aesthetics: "Among the Ibo the art of conversation is regarded very highly, and proverbs are the palm-oil with which words are eaten" (p. 10), while it ends with the counterbalancing linguistic perspective of the white district commissioner: "One of the most infuriating habits of these people was their love of superfluous words" (p. 189). The source of conflict is that the Ibo are an oral culture while the British comprise a literate one. Each finds the linguistic attitude of the other incomprehensible. The commissioner, who is writing a book about his African "experiences," does, of course, have the last word. The story of Okonkwo is to be written in English rather than preserved in the Ibo oral tradition.

For the Ibo, the coming of British colonization,[4] as well as the culturally anarchy which it forebodes, is marked by a breakdown in communication.[5] Despite the missionaries' claim to speak the language of the clan, their translator's humorous linguistic *faux pas* of saying "my buttocks" instead of "myself" (p. 135), as well as the Ibo's use of the term "kotma" which Achebe glosses as a word "not of Ibo origin but . . . a corruption of 'court messenger'" (p. 192), demonstrates the breakdown of language and the failed communication between the clan and its governors. Within the clan, people simply do not hear what is addressed to them, and the result is frequently the tense silence followed by misunderstanding. Obierika sums up this linguistic breakdown by noting that the clan "can no longer act as one. [The white man] has put a knife on the things that held us together and we have fallen apart" (p. 162). The last part of the lament serves to recall the line from Yeats's "The Second Coming" which provides the novel with its title. Within that poem, the first sign of the coming of such cultural anarchy is the parallel breakdown of communication: "The falcon cannot hear the falconer." Similarly, within Achebe's novel the bond which is severed by the advent of the missionaries is the linguistic identity which unites the Ibo as an nation possessed of a single vision and, hence, a culture.[6] Thus, during the farewell speeches made upon the end of Okonkwo's banishment, an elder of the clan states that he fears for the young because they "do not know what it is to speak with one voice" (p. 155). What the Ibo have come to lose are the words of their fathers—the proverbial traditions upon which their oral society is founded.[7] And, indeed, with its admonitions of "Blessed is he who forsakes his father and his mother for my sake. . . . Those that hear my words are my father and my mother" (p. 143), it is the new religion which has been responsible for that loss, for a fundamental tenet of the missionaries is that "Only the word of [their] God is true" (p. 147). Finally, for all his plans to stir his kinsmen's hearts with speeches at tribal council, Okonkwo, the novel's protagonist, is upon the arrival of the messengers of the New Dispensation "unable to utter a word" so that in the end there is only "utter silence" (p. 188). Thus, despite their previously valued tradition of great oratory, the tragic flaw which dooms the men of Umuofia is an ironic verbal impotence.

If the central conflict of the novel is, then, essentially one of survival between an oral and a literature culture, Achebe takes great care to capture the oral nature of Ibo society, if only to trace the tragic loss of this tradition. As with all oral cultures, the Ibo consistently demonstrates a love of language and a deep respect for those who use it well.[8] From the very first chapter, the importance of oratory is made manifest in the fashion in which Ogbuefi Ezeugo, a "powerful orator" (p. 14), holds sway over the clan with his exhortation to war with the neighboring Mbaino (p. 15). The measure of what has been lost to the men of Umuofia is put into relief through the startling contrast between the effective oratory of this opening council and the awkward silence into which the council of the penultimate chapter descends, for in the final council, the clan no longer speaks with "one voice," and there is no decision to take action.

In depicting what might be called the "pre-lapserian" state of the Ibo life, Achebe pays particular attention to the building blocks of that rhetoric or oratory. The world of the Ibo is clearly a world of ritual and ceremony which is, in turn, founded on a complex system of verbal etiquette—for the Ibo live under a strictly enforced set of rules concerning when to speak, how to speak, and to whom one may speak. The gods speak amongst themselves in their own "esoteric" (p. 84) language. When the gods speak to men, the rules are clearly defined (p. 95). When men speak to each other, they must follow the rules of speech

such as those set down for "Peace Week" (p. 32). Even the oft-
quoted speech of the creatures of the earth, so important as a
source of wisdom in Ibo proverbs, has its own rules of decorum.
Thus to the Ibo, speech, itself, is the thread which runs through
and binds together the various parts of a multivalent creation.

Moreover, all parts of that speaking and spoken to, living
cosmos have their proper names, the knowledge of which is an
important part of Ibo oral etiquette. Sometimes objects such as
snakes are deliberately called by the "wrong" name, such as
"string," lest they hear and respond to their proper names (p. 13).
Similarly, when one was called by name, it was the proper response in case the caller was an evil spirit (p. 42). Finally, as a
matter of protocol, spirits always addressed humans as "bodies"
(p. 86). What is important here is that in each case, the naming
function is predicated on a belief in the power of language to ex-
ercise control over and evoke a response from the objects which
it describes.

As the use of names suggests, linguistic etiquette among
the Ibo, as with most oral cultures, is characterized by a verbal
strategy of indirection rather than directness in speech—the very
quality of discourse which has already been noted to be a source
of particular chagrin to the District Commissioner. Within Ibo
speech, objects are not only called by names other than their own
but subject matter is often introduced by seemingly irrelevant
material. As with most of the linguistic traits of the Ibo, this
habit is established almost immediately within the novel and is
seen first in Okoye's attempt to remind Unoka of an outstanding
debt (p. 10) and in Okonkwo's plea for a loan of seed yams (p. 22).
However, such indirection is most clearly set forth in the account of Ofoedu's presentation of the news of the death of a
clansman and in the bargaining over the marriage terms of
Obierika's daughter. Rather than treat the matter which Ofoedu
has come to discuss, the men practice the ritual of the kola and
speak of it since despite the fact that "It was clear from the twin-
kling in his eyes that he had important news . . . it would be im-
polite to rush him" (p. 65). Similarly, the narrator tells of the
bridal bargaining by noting that, "As the men drank, they talked
about everything except the thing for which they had gathered"
(p. 69).

This deliberate lack of directness finds its source in more
than the conversational strategies of the Ibo but is reflected in
the structure and form of the language, itself, for the Ibo are fond

of compounding as a means of creation of new words as is, for example, seen in the fact that "the name for a corn cob with only a few scattered grains was eze-agadi-nwayi, or the teeth of an old woman" (p. 36). And as with this example, the chief aim of the Ibo speaker is often the evocation of verbal imagery through the creation of visual analogy rather than the attainment of verbal compactness. Similarly, as with many oral cultures, the Ibo demonstrate a great propensity for the use of analogy in much of their speech. Even the ordinary actions of men are compared to those of history and of legend. The sources or models of these analogies are as often animal as human, again reflecting the holistic world view of Ibo thought in which all things are seen to be interconnected. In the same fashion, much of the Ibo's speech, both ordinary and ceremonial, is clearly formulaic in nature, relying on the wealth of proverbial material which occurs throughout the novel. Already described in language typical of Ibo word-imagery as "the palm oil with which the words are eaten," such proverbs which punctuate most of the novel's dialogue occur some twenty-two times within the narrative,[9] and since their function is to preserve the collective wisdom of the clan, the growing doubts of the novel's protagonist concerning their truthfulness is an apt symbol of the gradual erosion of the clan's oral tradition.

Along with its wealth of proverbial material, *Things Fall Apart* also contains many other staples of folk oratory such as parables, folk tales, songs, legends and fables which appear to touch all aspects of Ibo life. The songs, for example, are the play time amusement of children (p. 52), a means of immortalizing the deeds of a young wrestler (p. 50), a way of preserving the eccentricities of an old, married couple (p. 66), a means of conveying proverbial wisdom (p. 52), and a humorous way of spreading a bit of popular wit (p. 112). The stories range in scope from the local tale of the near legendary opulence of one man's feast (p. 38) to the tale of how the trickster tortoise received the markings on his shell (pp. 91-93). As with the proverbs, each of these elements of the folk speech of the Ibo furthers the habit of verbal elaboration and indirection, and of the many examples of their use within the tale, one of the clearest is seen in the account of the murder of the missionary by the Mbanta. First, the facts of the matter are told as they are known (pp. 128-129). This account is followed by the proverb, "Never kill a man who says nothing" (p. 129), which is intended to explain the larger, abstract lesson to be learned from the tale. Finally, an even longer fable about a mother kite is introduced as a means of explaining, or at least elaborating the proverb (p. 130).

Ironically it is this deeply ingrained love of song and fable and poetry which attracts the men of the village to the new religion which the missionaries bring to Umuofia. Although unmoved by the "logic" of the missionaries, the men of the village are "enthralled" by "one of those gay and rollicking tunes of the evangelism which had the power of plucking at silent and dusty chords in the heart of the Ibo men" (p. 136). Among the villagers listening to those songs and stories is the son of Okonkwo: "It was not the mad logic of the Trinity that captivated him. He did not understand it. It was the poetry of the new religion, something felt in the marrow" (p. 137). Yet despite initial appearances, there is a great deal more of "mad logic" to the new religion of the missionaries than there is of poetry. Although the missionaries, in their initial attempts to convert the clan, make a pretense of speaking the language of the villagers (p. 134), it is clear from their mistranslations and linguistic *faux pas* that they do not. In fact, what is clear is that the missionaries bring not only a new language but an entirely different linguistic aesthetic.

The chief quality of Ibo speech was its expansiveness—achieved, as we have seen, through the use of elaboration, repetition, and analogy. With its joy in multiplicity, the language of the Ibo is essentially centrifugal, beginning with a single idea and working outward to its many forms of expression, as we see in the use of both the proverb and the fable in the first account of the missionaries' arrival at Mbanta. In contrast, the chief quality of the speech patterns of the missionaries is its proclivity for reduction rather than expansion. Nowhere is this tendency more plainly seen than in the novel's final paragraph in which the Commissioner considers the book which he intends to write about his African experiences.

> Every day brought him some new material. The story of this man who had killed the messenger and hanged himself would make interesting reading. One could almost write a whole chapter on him. Perhaps not a whole chapter but a reasonable paragraph, at any rate. There was so much else to include, and one must be firm in cutting out details.   (p. 191)

The irony is, of course, immediately apparent: the life which it has taken Achebe some two hundred pages to chronicle is, in the course of three scant sentences, reduced to a mere "reasonable" paragraph in the mind of the commissioner. The richness of Ibo story-telling, evident in the legendary account of Okonkwo's wrestling match with "Amalinze the Cat" in the very first paragraph, stands in stark contrast to the almost painful brevity of the treatise which the commissioner outlines in the novel's final paragraph. This tendency towards linguistic reductionism on the part of the commissioner is not, however, a matter of personal style or idiosyncrasy but is, rather, a verbal characteristic of all of the non-Ibo speaking characters in the novel. The linguistic brevity of the English speakers is seen in their monosyllabic names, Smith and Brown, especially in light of the attention given to the expansiveness of the polysyllabic, compounded names of the Ibo.

Indeed, in contrast to the verbal expansiveness of the Ibo, Brown appears to be the very embodiment of linguistic reductionism. For Brown and the rest of the missionaries, something is either true, or it is not—hence, their insistence that "Only the word of our God is true" (p. 147). According to Mr. Brown, "the leaders of the land in the future would be men and women who had learned to read and write" (p. 166).[10] The oral culture must be given up in order to gain a place in the new literate one. One is either among the community of the saved who believe in an exact doctrine or one is not. There is for the missionaries no middle way, only "The Way." In contrast, the Ibo live in a world filled with many voices, all of which can speak the truth. Thus, within a single conversation on a single page, proverbial wisdom is successively taken from the mouths of "the lizard," "Eneke the bird," and "our fathers" (p. 24).

Finally, if the clash between these divergent cultures is clearly defined and the two sides neatly set apart, that conflict finds its embodiment in the person of Okonkwo—the novel's central character who, despite his claim to be the only one willing to fight for the clan's cultural survival, is actually a man who unknowingly stands midway between the two cultures. Rejecting both the past, in his father and the future, in his son, Okonkwo can really speak to neither and, himself, becomes a symbol for the linguistic breakdown which occurs in the novel. Like a modern day Billy Budd, his fatal flaw is his stammer (pp. 8-18), his inability to communicate. Already described as "not a man of many words" (p. 130), Okonkwo consistently wishes to act rather than speak, to fight the fight of the clan in a fashion which violates the principles of the culture which he hopes to save. The demon which he is fighting is, in the end, his own reflection, for in his brusqueness of speech and impatience with verbal indirection he possesses many of the characteristics of the missionaries who are his mortal enemies.

As such, the novel's chief character stands at the very edge of the chaos which heralds the coming of a new dispensation, much like the terrified persona in "The Second Coming." Interestingly enough, this very type of terror in the face of change has been described by Achebe in the context of linguistic change, for he has noted elsewhere that "when language is seriously interfered with . . . be it from mere incompetence or worse, from malice, horrors can descend again on mankind."[11] In his portrayal of the cultural collision between the Ibo and the British missionaries who come to colonize Umuofia, Achebe has produced a fictionalized, sociolinguistic study which demonstrates his linguistic principles and evokes that very horror as the direct result of the cultural disintegration which necessarily follows the abandonment of linguistic identity. In the end, the hieroglyph of the sphinx is to be displaced by that of the rough beast. The oral culture of the Nigerian Ibo is destined to be subsumed into that of the literate English.

Notes

[1] All textual citations are taken from Chinua Achebe, *Things Fall Apart* (New York: Fawcett, 1978).

[2] For Achebe's thoughts concerning language as a medium for the expression of ideas and especially concerning the question of English as a suitable medium for "African" literature, see Chinua Achebe, "The African Writer and the English Language" in Chinua Achebe, *Morning Yet on Creation Day* (Garden City: Anchor Press, 1975), pp. 91-104.

[3] See Chinua Achebe, "Language and the Destiny of Man" in *Morning Yet on Creation Day*, pp. 47-59.

[4] For a detailed account of British colonial policy and its implications in Nigeria, see John Hatch, *Nigeria* (Chicago: Henry Regnery Co., 1970), especially p. 192 for a discussion of the British lack of understanding of the Ibo. Also see Elizabeth Isichei, *The Ibo People and the Europeans: The Genesis of a Relationship, to 1906* (New York: St. Martin's, 1973).

[5] See N. Djangone-Bi, "Cultural Change in Achebe's Novels," *LHY* 21 (198)), 156-166.

[6] For Achebe's view of the role of language in such "oral" cultures, see Achebe, "Destiny." Also see Isichei pp. 27-42 for a discussion of Ibo oral tradition in regard to what it reveals about Ibo culture.

[7] See Chukwuma Okoye, "Achebe: The Literary Function of Proverbs and Proverbial Sayings in Two Novels," *Lore & L.* 2 (1979), 45-63.

[8] M. M. Green, in *Ibo Village Affairs* (New York: Frederick A. Praeger, (1964) notes the importance of language as a factor in Ibo identity (pp. 5-6, 12). Also see Hatch, p. 76.

[9] See pp. 14, 22, 23, 24, 28, 29, 59, 74, 68, 70, 96, 118, 129-143, 154, 165 and 187.

[10] For the importance of education in the politics and strategies of the British missionaries in Nigeria, see Hatch, pp. 190-192.

[11] Achebe, "Destiny," p. 59.

Sophisticated Primitivism: The Syncretism of Oral and Literate Modes in Achebe's *Things Fall Apart*

Abdul Janmohamed

I

The use of the English language and literary forms by African (and other Third World) writers must be understood in the context of a larger social, political, and ideological dialogue between British, and particularly colonialist, literature on the one hand and the ex-colonized writers of the Third World on the other. Faced by the colonialist denigration of his past and present culture and consequently motivated by a desire to negate the prior European negation of indigenous society, the African writer embarks on a program of regaining the dignity of self and society by representing them, in the best instances, in a manner that he considers unidealized but more authentic. This negative dialogue transcends the literary polemic about authentic "images" of Africans and manifests itself in an opposition of forms as well: thus, for instance, Chinua Achebe is drawn to realism partly in order to counter the "racial romances" of Joyce Cary.[1] However, some critics have argued that the African end of this dialogue is unable to negate colonialist literature totally precisely because it relies on the English language to do so. The question that underlies this criticism is indeed an important one: can African experience be adequately represented through the alien media (ones that were fashioned to codify an entirely different encounter with reality) of the colonizers' language and literary forms or will these media inevitably alter the nature of African experience in significant ways? But the question cannot be answered very easily. While the ideological sentiment behind this criticism is perfectly understandable and laudable, the

critics who want Third World writers to abandon European languages and forms have not concretely examined the results of
the contemporary syncretic literatures of the Third World.
Whatever answers are ultimately given to the underlying question, the concrete evidence must be scrutinized first.   Thus I
would like to bracket temporarily the controversy about English
in order to examine, in this essay, an issue that, one can argue,
has causal priority: how is the encounter between the predomi-
nantly *oral* cultures of Africa and the literate cultures of the colonizer represented and mediated by anglophone African fiction?
Is such fiction, which, to stress the obvious, is literate and written in English, able to do justice to the phenomenology of
oral/mythic cultures, which is radically different from that of
chirographic cultures? From an ideological viewpoint we must
also inquire whether or not the adoption of the alien language
makes a significant contribution to the negative dialogic relation
between African and English literatures.

The African writer's very decision to use English as his
medium is engulfed by ironies, paradoxes, and contradictions.
He writes in English because he was born in a British colony and
can receive formal education only in English. More significantly, however, he is compelled to master and use English because of the prevailing ideological pressures within the colonial
system. At the surface level, these manifest themselves through
the ethnocentric narcissism of the European colonialists who
will only recognize the other as a "civilized" human being if he
recreates himself in their image by adopting the appropriate
European language as well as literary forms. This applies to all
aspects of culture and politics: for instance, the granting of "independence" itself is contingent upon the adoption of some version of Western parliamentary democracy. At a deeper level the
insistence that the colonies accept European forms, values, and
beliefs represents a deliberate, if subconscious, strategy to ensure
an unproblematic change from dominant to hegemonic colonialism. "Independence" marks the transition from the dominant phase, where "consent" of the dominated is obtained by
direct coersion, to the hegemonic phase, where "consent" is pro-
cured through the ideological formation of the dominated subject. Thus the adoption of European languages, and subse-
quently European values, beliefs, etc., by the native remains crucial to the hegemonic transfer which generates, as by-products,
anglophone, francophone, etc., Third World writers who may or

may not be involved in a negative dialogue with European literature. (Some writers, such as V. S. Naipaul, who has clearly
adopted the "author function" of the colonizer, are more inclined to represent a version of the colonialist viewpoint.) Finally, a potential writer from a British colony is induced to use
English because it is an intimate part of a powerful society that
will control all technological and cultural development in the
foreseeable future.

Yet the decision to use English produces a contradiction
between, on the one hand, the unconscious and subconscious
psychic formations of most Third World writers, determined by
the indigenous languages, and, on the other hand, the more superficial, conscious formation, determined by the formal, public
function of English is most colonies. The problem is compounded by the fact that, unlike English, most African languages
were non-literate and that the noetic structures of these oral cultures are significantly different from those of chirographic ones.
The African writer who uses English, then, is faced at some level
with the paradox of representing the experience of oral cultures
through literate language and forms. Chinua Achebe, on whose
first novel I shall concentrate, is subconsciously aware of this
problem and has depicted in his fiction not only the material,
political, and social destruction of indigenous societies caused by
colonization but also the subtle annihilation of the conservative,
homeostatic oral culture by the colonialists' introduction of literacy. Thus his novels not only depict the materiality of the destroyed and destroying worlds, but as chirographic representa-
tions of oral cultures they also become simultaneous agents of
the preservation and destruction of the oral world. The style
and structure of *Things Fall Apart*, I shall argue, do encode the
phenomenology of oral cultures and thereby create a new syncretic form and contribute to the negative dialectics by deterritorializing, to some extent, the English language and the novelistic
form.

II

The differences between oral and chirographic cultures
have been articulated most thoroughly and systematically by Jack
Goody and Walter J. Ong,[2] and the following, somewhat

schematic summary of these differences is based on their modulated analyses. Goody correctly emphasized the fact that traditional anthropological formulations of the differences between these kinds of cultures through the binary and ethnocentric categories such as civilized/savage, rational/irrational, scientific/mythic, hot/cold/ etc., are essentially Manichean, that is they tend to valorize morally one term at the expense of the other and to characterize the differences as being qualitative, categorical, and ontological rather than quantitative, material, and technological. Both Goody and Ong insist that the essential differences between these cultures can be explained through a scrutiny of literacy and its effects. The point, as Goody puts it, is that the "relationship between modes of thought and the modes for the production and reproduction of thought . . . [lies] at the heart of the unexplained but not inexplicable differences that so many writers have noted,"[3] that changes in the modes of production and reproduction of thought, i.e., (alphabetic) literacy and later printing, are bound to affect the very content and modes of thought.

Literacy, by isolating thought on a written surface, tends to alienate language, knowledge, and world in positive and productive ways. When an utterance "is put in writing it can be inspected in much greater detail, in its parts as well as in its whole, backwards as well as forwards, out of context as well as in its setting; in other words, it can be subjected to a quite different type of scrutiny and critique than is possible with purely verbal communication. Speech is no longer tied to an 'occasion'; it becomes timeless. Nor is it attached to a person; on paper, it becomes more abstract, more depersonalized."[4] This kind of scrutiny eventually leads to the development of syllogistic and other forms of analysis. By allowing one to record events as they occur, to store them for long periods of time, and to recall them in their original forms, literacy eventually builds up a dense representation of the past and thus leads to the development of historical consciousness and secular teleology. The availability of a dense past and more sophisticated analytic tools in turn encourages greater reflexivity and self-scrutiny. One must emphasize again that oral cultures are unable to develop these characteristics not because of some genetic, racial or cultural inferiority but simply because they lack the proper tool, namely literacy. Yet in the absence of these essential features of chirographic societies, the phenomenology of oral cultures tends to be characterized by

the following traits: it defines meaning and value contextually
rather than abstractly; it is conservative and homeostatic; its
universe is defined by mythic rather than historical consciousness; it valorizes collectively rather than individually; and it is
dominated by a totalizing imperative.

Oral cultures tend to define concepts through situational,
operational frames of reference that are minimally abstract.
Ideas are comprehended either through their concrete manifes-
tations or through their context, but rarely in terms of other abstract ideas; lexis is controlled through direct semantic ratification, through experience rather than logical definition. Writing,
on the other hand, creates a context-free or "autonomous" discourse. Written words are no longer directly bound up with reality; they become separate "things," abstracted from the flow of
speech, shedding their close entailment with action and context.

Since the conservation of conceptualized knowledge in
oral cultures depends on memory, that which is not memorized
through repetition soon disappears. This mnemonic need establishes a highly traditionalist or conservative set of mind that
tends to inhibit experimentation and innovation. On the other
hand, the mind in chirographic cultures, freed from this
mnemonic constraint, is not only able to experiment but, perhaps more significantly, to record and build on innovations and
changes. Consequently, oral societies tend to adopt a protective
attitude towards their epistemological and phenomenological
categories and established theories and practices, whereas literate
societies, particularly after they have embarked on a program of
"scientific" inquiry, are more sceptical, critical, and analytic. The
former tend to systematize and valorize belief, the latter, doubt.
A corollary of the conserving function of the oral community is
its homeostatic imperative, that is, its decision to maintain the
equilibrium of the present by sloughing off memories which no
longer have present relevance. The present needs of oral societies constantly impose their economy on past remembrances,
and past events that are released from memory can never be re-
cuperated in non-literate cultures.

The inability of oral cultures to document this past in a
systematic and detailed manner, of course, means that they are
dominated not by a historical but a mythic consciousness. As an
account of origins, myth differs from history in that its claims
cannot be verified with anything like the kind of accuracy available to literate societies. Based on this fundamental difference,

Ernst Cassirer makes further distinctions between oral/mythic and scientific/historical consciousness that seem to be accurate but that are unfortunately formulated in fundamentally ethnocentric, Manichean terms.[5] However, at the very least, one can say that because the noetic economy of oral/mythic consciousness is not burdened by the needs of ratification it is able to develop a more fluid symbolic exchange system. This fluidity not only facilitates the enactment of the central teleological imperative of oral cultures, i.e., to maintain a constant homeostatic balance, but also permits the development of a specific relation between collectivity and individuality (weighted towards the former) and the economy and configuration of its totalizing imperative.

Communication in oral societies necessarily takes place in "primary group" relationships, that is, through intimate face-to-face contact. The result of this "intimate association, psychologically, is a certain fusion of individualities in a common whole, so that one's very self, for many purposes at least, is the common life and purpose of the group."[6] Thus oral cultures tend to valorize collectivity over individuality and to create "individual" personality structures that are in fact communal and externalized, not inclined towards introspection. The externalized individual, then, is easily managed through the symbolic exchanges involved in communal ritual and practices. Writing and reading, on the other hand, are solitary achievements that tend, at least momentarily, to throw the psyche back on itself, and the knowledge that one's thoughts, when they are committed to writing, can endure in time encourages the emergence and recognition of individuality.

According to Ong, sight (and hence writing) isolates, while sound (and hence speech) incorporates. Whereas sight situates the observer outside what he views, at a distance, sound pours into the hearer; while sight is unidirectional, sound is enveloping. The centering action of sound affects man's sense of the cosmos. For oral cultures, the cosmos is an ongoing event with man at its centre. Man is the *umbilicus mundi*. In such societies, where the word has its existence only in sound, the phenomenology of sound enters deeply into a human being's feel for existence. All the characteristics of oral cultures discussed above relate intimately to the unifying and centralizing effect of sound. If we add to this tendency the fact that, in the absence of the analytic categories that are predicated on writing, oral cultures must conceptualize and verbalize all their knowledge with more or less close reference to the human lifeworld, assimilating the alien, objective world to the more immediate, familiar interaction of human beings, then we begin to glimpse the totalizing imperative of oral cultures. In such societies words, ideas, and reality are intrinsically bound; they are part of the same continuum. There is little distinction made between the pragmatic and non-pragmatic, the phenomenal and the numeral. All mundane reality is impregnated with spiritual significance and the entire cosmos inheres in the most insignificant object; metonymy and metaphor, as essential phenomenological and epistemological structures, are more deeply integral to the oral consciousness than they are to the chirographic mind. If man is the centre of the fluid symbolic economy of such a society and if such a universe is conceptualized through its humanization, then potentially man has total control of it if only he knows the correct formulas and practices. In such a culture an "individual" can easily become an emblem of the desires and conflicts of the entire society, and this characteristic is, of course, important for the production of heroic, epic narratives.

Narrative is more functional in oral cultures than in others for two reasons. Since oral cultures cannot generate abstract or scientific categories for coding experience, they use stories of human (or anthropomorphized animal) action to organize, store, and communicate knowledge and experience. Second, such societies use narratives to bind a great deal of cultural signification that exists in less durable verbal forms. Thus, for example, oral narrative will often incorporate folktales, orations, genealogies, proverbs, etc. Unlike the linear or pyramidal plots of chirographic narratives, which are predicated on careful written revision, the plots of oral narratives are episodic and non-sequential: the narrator will report a situation and only much later explain, often in great detail, how it came to be. Yet, as Ong insists, this is not due to the narrator's desire to hasten into the midst of action. Such an interpretation is a product of literate cultures which assume that a linear plot has been deliberately scrambled. The episodic oral "plot" is really a product of the narrator *remembering* the story in a curious public way—remembering not a memorized "text" or a verbatim succession of words but themes, episodes, and formulae, which, along with the entire story, are *already known* by the audience as part of the culture's myths.

The narrative thus simultaneously exists as a public and private event: "as a traditional and external fact, the oral tale is foreseeable; as a literary fact (poetic, individual experience, etc.), the produced oral text has an internal finality that finds support in the foreseeable." The relation between the public (already known) and private (a specific retelling) version of a narrative is dialectical. The narrative is a potentiality that exists prior to the productive act of the narrator, while a specific performance of the story is a variation and an innovation that refers to the potentiality just as *parole* refers to *langue*.[7] Thus creativity as well as aesthetic appositeness lie in choosing a formal element (proverb, folktale, etc.) and in (re)arranging of episodes in a plot sequence in ways that are appropriate to the specific narrative context. The oral narrative, then, is "situational" in a double sense: it proceeds episodically, that is, it reports a situation that is modified or explained much later and apparently at random; and the specific performance is partly determined by the narrative situation, that is, by the interaction between audience and narrator. The "scrambled" sequence of an oral narrative, with its necessary recapitulations and postponed amplifications and explanations, results in repetition or copia as one of its characteristic features. Yet repetition must not be mistaken for redundancy (a term that Ong uses as a synonym). As Harold Scheub has shown, it has an aesthetic function; oral narratives deliberately cultivate and intensify repetitions in order to realize their cumulative effects.[8] We may add to this the possibility that the neotic function of repetition may be to reinforce the homeostatic imperative of oral cultures because well-modulated repetition would have the effect of recreating the balance of an already known, ordered, controlled, and rhythmically harmonious universe. A specific aesthetic corollary of copia that also characterizes oral narrative is the predominance of parataxis, both at the level of syntax and that of the larger narrative units—formulas, episodes, etc.

The neotic economy of oral narratives also tends to generate heroic figures, not for romantic or deliberately didactic reasons but for more basic ones. In the first place, outsized characters are more memorable than the "ordinary" individuals of literate texts, and this is, of course, an important consideration for cultures without texts. In addition to encouraging triumphalism this economy also prefers heroic "flat characters" because around them can be organized the most significant elements of the cul-

ture: in fact these character serve as the emblems of the culture
and can be used to manage all kinds of non-narrative elements
embedded in the story. Psychic and social interiority, the
"roundedness" of well-developed chirographic characters, is
rarely a significant concern of these narratives. Since such narratives emblemize, through the heroic figure, the totality of the
culture and since the formal features of such stories evoke the
noetic structures of an oral universe, the very performance of an
oral narrative is itself a profoundly totalizing act. As Ngal insists, such narratives incorporate and commune with the core of
the culture and evoke a "sense of belonging to a common history."[9] I think it might be more accurate to say that such narratives allow the narrator and the audience to (re)integrate themselves with the totality and the totalizing imperative of their culture. As Goody points out and as Ruth Finnegan's study illustrates,[10] while the content of these narratives can vary widely,
the formal characteristics invariably remain constant.

                                III

        Chinua Achebe's style in *Things Fall Apart* is consonant
with the oral culture that he represents. In fact, the congruence
between the style, elements of the narrative structure, and characterization, on the one hand, and the nature of the culture represented, on the other, account for the success of the novel: because Achebe is able to capture the flavour of an oral society in
his style and narrative organization, *Things Fall Apart* is able to
represent successfully the specificity of a culture alien to most
Western readers.
        His sentence structure is on the whole paratactic; it
achieves its effect largely through juxtaposition, addition, and
aggregation. Consider the opening paragraph of the novel:

> Okonkwo was well known throughout the nine vil-
> lages and even beyond. His fame rested on solid per-
> sonal achievements. As a young man of eighteen he
> had brought honor to his village by throwing Amalinze
> the Cat. Amalinze was the great wrestler who for
> seven years was unbeaten, from Umuofia to Mbaino. He
> was called the Cat because his back would never touch
> the earth. It was this man that Okonkwo threw in a
> fight. . . .[11]

In spite of the glaring opportunities for consolidating the short, simple sentences and subordinating some of them as modifying clauses, thereby emphasizing the more important elements, Achebe refuses to do so precisely because syntactic subordination is more characteristic of chirographic representation than it is of oral speech. The desired effect of this parataxis, which, as we will see, is echoed in the narrative organization of the novel, is the creation of a flat surface: since one fact is not subordinated to another more important one, everything exists on the same plane and is equally important. Of course, as one proceeds through the novel one begins to see that all the details coalesce around the heroic figure of Okonkwo, but while reading any one paragraph or chapter the initial effect is one of equivalence. This style and its effects, it must be emphasized, are deliberate. As Achebe himself has shown by comparing a more abstract and hypotactic version of a paragraph from *Arrow of God* with the concrete and paratactic original, the former is inappropriate for the protagonist of the novel and his context.[12] The deliberateness of this style is also emphasized by its contrast with passages of oratory at political gatherings, funerals, and other formal occasions when the language, though still paratactic, is characterized by greater rhetorical formality. For instance, Uchendu's avuncular advice to Okonkwo is not only very dramatic and punctuated effectively with rhetorical questions but is also tightly structured according to the demands of the logic of his argument (*TFA*, pp. 122-125).

The effect of parataxis, however, is modulated by the repetition of various kinds of details. Significant facts keep resurfacing like a leitmotif: for example, Okonkwo's achievement of fame through wrestling is introduced in the first paragraph on page seven, then repeated again on pages eleven and twenty-nine, and finally the narrator devotes an entire chapter (*TFA*, pp. 46-50) to the importance of this sport in Igbo culture. At times virtually identical statements are repeated. Chapter three begins with the following statement: "Okonkwo did not have the start in life which many young men usually had. He did not inherit a barn from his father. There was no barn to inherit" (*TFA*, p. 19). This is followed by a two-page depiction of his father's laziness, which ends with "With a father like Unoka, Okonkwo did not have the start in life which many young men had. He neither inherited a barn nor a title, nor even a young wife" (*TFA*, p. 21). Playing against the flat surface of the paratactic prose, such repetitions create a sense of rhythm and valorize some facts above others. This does produce a kind of subordination, but the fact that these repetitions are embedded in a flat narrative surface implies that they must be understood in terms of the overall situation; without the context these facts lose their value. In this novel significance is a function of recurrence, not of logical analytic valorization. The importance of context is illustrated by the fact that meaning of complex concepts is defined by reference to concrete situations rather than abstract elaboration. Thus, for example, *efulefu*, a worthless individual, is defined as follows: "The imagery of an *efulefu* in the language of the clan was a man who sold his machete and wore the sheath to battle" (*TFA*, p. 133). Or the apparent contradiction between the two definitions of *chi* as they appear on pages twenty-nine and thirty-three is explained by the context, which makes it clear that the *chi* is in agreement with the self when one is in harmony with oneself and the entire culture but that it becomes antagonistic when one is alienated from self and society. Though repetition and contextual definition modify the flat surface of the narrative, they do not, as we shall see later, create a distinction between background and foreground. Rather their function is to create a series of patterns on that surface.

Elements of the narrative structure and organization repeat and amplify, on a different register, the same effects. Yet the narrative, like the style, is a product of a double consciousness, of a syncretic combination of chirographic and oral techniques. Just as the style represents in writing the syntax and thought patterns of oral cultures, so the narrative operates on two levels: in its novelistic form the story of Okonkwo is unique and historical, yet it is told as if it were a well-known myth. The narrative acknowledges the latter fact in its opening sentence: "Okonkwo was well known throughout the nine villages and even beyond" (*TFA*, p. 7). The story of his poverty "was told in Umuofia" (*TFA*, p. 19), and that of Ikemefuna's sacrifice "is still told to this day" (*TFA*, p. 16). Similarly other aspects of this narrative manifest themselves as circulating oral tales, and the white colonizers first appear to the hero in the form of stories. The reader is left with an impression that these tales are loosely connected but that the narrator of *Things Fall Apart* will (re)stitch them in his own unique order. However, even though the "myth" about Okonkwo and his family is common knowledge it has to be told (and heard) as if for the first time. Thus, for example, after introducing the fact of Nwoye's apostasy and after depicting for several pages the first encounter between the Christian missionaries and the Igbos, Achebe returns to Nwoye's conversation with the following sentences: "But there was a young lad who had been captivated [by Christianity]. His name was Nwoye, Okonkwo's first son" (*TFA*, p. 137). This presentation of the apostasy, the name of the character, and his parentage as if for the first time is not due, we must assume, to narrative amnesia. Rather it is a part of the process of remembering in a public way, a product of returning, after a "digression" and in the absence of a text, to the facts. This technique of public remembrance, which seems to annoy many "literate" readers, accounts for the pervasive pattern wherein Achebe introduces a topic and then repeatedly returns to it in order to explain it piecemeal (see, for example, the series of reversions to the story of Ikemefuna until he is finally executed in chapter seven). Aspects of this pattern can be accounted for by the need to foreshadow, which is common to both chirographic and oral narratives. The overall effect of this pattern of postponements and reversions, of the juxtapositions of central themes and "digressions" is to create an interlocking mosaic of episodes out of which the significance of the story gradually emerges.

By proceeding through public remembrance the narrative makes ample use of periphrasis, which, according to Achebe, is a highly prized technique of Igbo conversion: "Among the Igbo the act of conversation is regarded very highly, and proverbs are the palm-oil with which words are eaten. Okoye was a great talker and he spoke for a long time, skirting round the subject and then hitting it finally" (*TFA*, pp. 10-11). Like Okoye, the narrator skirts around his subject but carefully maintains certain ambiguities (which we shall examine later). The first chapter provides a good example of this narrative circularity. It covers the following subjects in that order: Okonkwo's fame, wrestling ability, personality, his father's character and indebtedness, Okonkwo's shame, his struggle for recognition and wealth, and his consequent custody of Ikemefuna, and the latter's destiny. In this spiral the chapter encapsulates the entire plot of part one of *Things Fall Apart*. The other twelve chapters of part one explore all of these issues in much greater detail, but not in the same order. In fact, the topics are thoroughly scrambled and a great deal of space is devoted to the depiction of the central events in the life of an agrarian community—planting, harvesting, etc., and

the various festivals that accompany them—as well as rituals
such as marriages, funerals, convening of the legal-spiritual
court of the *egwugwus*, etc. Out of the one-hundred-and-eigh-
teen pages that comprise part one of the novel only about eight
are devoted, strictly speaking, to the development of the plot.[13]
The narrator is therefore anxious to represent the cultural "background" as much as the heroic figure, and in doing so he is able
to depict the core of his culture and show that Okonkwo is one
of its heroic representatives. Having thus depicted the interconnected totality of the culture and having established Okonkwo as
its emblem in part one of the novel, the narrator, who in keeping with the already known narrative, is sensitively aware of the
arrival of the destructive colonialists and their chirographic culture, changes the organization and the pace of the second and
third parts of the novel: the plot now follows a more rigorous
and increasingly urgent chronological and causal pattern until it
ends suddenly with Okonkwo fixed as a minor detail in a minor
book of vast chirographic culture. The elaborate oral narrative
that has been sustained throughout the novel is startlingly displaced by a casual, "objective" paragraph about Okonkwo in the
District Officer's book.

    However, the narrative principle that leads to this dra-
matic end is not causality but contiguity. As the outline of the
first chapter illustrates, most often the narrative proceeds
through association of subject matter. At times, however, the
association focuses explicitly on a word, such as "household,"
which provides the link between the three parts of the second
chapter. Achebe's studied avoidance of causality as an organiza-
tional principle is consonant with the epistemology of oral cultures, which have not developed their analytic capacities because
they do not have access to literacy. The subsequent dependence
of the plot on contiguity results in parataxis at the narrative
level, which in turn reinforces the flat surface of the novel.

    Nowhere is the decision to preserve this flatness, the re-
fusal to emphasize the divisions between foreground and background, between the phenomenal and the numenal more apparent than in the narrator's management of the border between
the secular and the sacred. In pure oral cultures such a distinction does not exist, but Achebe and his novel both exist in the
margins of chirographic and oral cultures. The author is thus
challenged with the unenviable task of ensuring that his characters do not seem foolish because they believe in the absence of

that border while he is obliged to acknowledge it for the same reason. Achebe meets this challenge by endowing his characters and narrator with a double consciousness. At the beginning of the legal-spiritual court where *egwugwus* first appear, the narrator tells us that "Okonkwo's wives, and perhaps other women as well, might have noticed that the second *egwugwu* had the springy walk of Okonkwo. And they might also have noticed that Okonkwo was not among the titled men and elders who sat behind the row of *egwugwu*. But if they thought these things they kept them to themselves. The *egwugwu* with the springy walk was one of the dead fathers of the clan. He looked terrible. . ." (*TFA*, p. 85). Thus the narrator demonstrates for us the double consciousness—the awareness of the border and its deep repression—of the characters, while admitting to the reader that Okonkwo is "dressed up" as an *egwugwu* and then proceeding to deny that admission (i.e., Okonkwo "*was* one of the dead fathers. . .", italics added). By maintaining a deliberate ambiguity, a double consciousness in keeping with the syncretism of a written narrative about an oral culture, the narrator refuses to emphasize either the chirographic/scientific or the oral/mythic viewpoint, thereby once again reinforcing the flat surface.

The same effect is obtained through the monotony of the narrative voice and the timeless aura of the story. The voice remains unchanged even when it is retelling a folktale recounted by one of the characters (e.g., *TFA*, p. 91). The chronology is extremely vague; temporal locations are designated only by phrases such as "many years ago," "years ago," "as old as the clan itself," "the worst year in living memory," and so on (*TFA*, pp. 7, 9, 15, 25). The only specific periods in the novel are associated with ritual punishment: Ikemefuna's three years in Okonkwo's custody and Okonkwo's seven years in exile. Otherwise the novel is as timeless as one with a historical setting (indicated most obviously by the arrival of English colonialists to this area, around 1905) can be: the narrative, as an aggregation of already known, circulating stories, exists in seamless mythic rather than segmented historical time.

Characterization too is a product of the oral aesthetic economy; it is, however, more clearly modified by the historicizing demands of the (chirographic) novelistic imperatives. As Bakhtin points out, in the historicizing move from the epic to the novel, it is "precisely the zone of contact with an inconclusive present (and consequently with the future) that creates the necessity of [the] incongruity of man with himself. There always remains in him unrealized potential and unrealized demands." Unlike the tragic or epic hero, who can be incarnated quite satisfactorily within the existing sociohistorical categories, the "individual" in the novel invariably raises the issue of his inadequacy to his fate and situation, and thereby calls into question the efficacy of the existing sociohistorical categories. The movement from the monochronic and totalized world of the epic to the historicized and dialogic world of the novel also leads to the disintegration of the individual in other ways: "A crucial tension develops between the external and the internal man, and as a result the subjectivity of the individual becomes an object of experimentation and representation. . . ."[14] *Things Fall Apart* is delicately poised at the transition from the epic (oral) to the novel (chirographic). In keeping with its oral origins, Achebe's novel entirely lacks the tension between internal and external man. Although Okonkwo's repression of the "feminine" emotions and Nwoyo's revulsion towards the discarding of twins and the execution of Ikemefuna are so crucial to the plot and the meaning of the novel, Achebe never explores them as dense interiorities (as a contemporary western writer would have). Rather he stays on the flat surface and represents the emotions through concrete metaphors. Consider, for example, Okonkwo's "mediation" of his son's apostasy. As he contemplates the incredulity of his son's action, Okonkwo, whose nickname is "Roaring Flame," gazes into the fire in his hut. The narrator finally presents the results of the ruminations as follows: "[Okonkwo] sighed heavily, and as if in sympathy the smoldering log also sighed. And immediately Okonkwo's eyes were opened and he saw the whole matter clearly. Living fire begets cold, impotent ash. He sighed again, deeply" (*TFA*, p. 143). From our viewpoint, the crucial aspect of this procedure is that Achebe chooses to represent interiority only through its concrete, material manifestation or reflection. Similarly, Nwoye's revulsion is represented through metaphors of physical sensation: when confronted with Ikemefuna's death "something seemed to give way inside him, like the snapping of a tightened bow" (*TFA*, p. 59). Thus, unlike Wole Soyinka's *The Interpreters*, *Things Fall Apart* refuses to "experiment" with the representation of subjectivity in a way that is familiar to contemporary Western readers.

However, the externality of representation does not mean that Okonkwo lacks subjectivity. The reader is made fully aware of the pride and anger with which the hero attempts to mask his shame and fear. In fact, the narrative focuses on the binary relationship of these emotions to the point where other aspects of the hero's psyche are ignored. Thus in keeping with the tradition of oral narrative Okonkwo remains a relatively flat character, whose efficacy must be judged not according to the criteria of some vague realistic notion of "roundness" but rather in terms of his twofold narrative function. First, he is an emblem of his culture. Through his mundane preoccupations and tribulations—his involvement in harvesting, planting, building houses, weddings, funerals, legal and spiritual rituals, etc.—we are allowed to penetrate the interiority of the Igbo culture before the arrival of British colonizers. Consequently when he commits suicide—which not only cuts him off from his ancestors but which is also the product of a complicated alienation from the principle of the continuity of ancestral lineage (he rejects his father, kills his foster son and drives away his real son)—his death leaves us with the feeling of massive cultural destruction, of an end of traditional Igbo culture. His second, ideological function is tied to the first; his shame and pride are also emblematic: the former represents the shame among the colonized by the colonizers' rhetoric about savagery and the latter reflects the resurgence in the African's pride in the moral efficacy of his culture as he understands it. For if Achebe introduces us to traditional Igbo culture through Okonkwo, he is doing so in order to show that it was civilized and, by extension, that the colonized individual need not be ashamed of his past. Yet in the process of using Okonkwo as an emblem Achebe also accedes to novelistic pressures. The transformation of Okonkwo from a heroic figure to an insignificant detail in a paragraph about savage custom is clearly a deflationary movement that raises questions about his potentiality and his adequacy to his situation. The novel is content neither with leaving Okonkwo as a completely stylized heroic figure nor with the impulse to idealize traditional Igbo culture. The reflexivity of the novel manifests itself through the dialogic relation between Okonkwo and his friend Obierika. While the former, driven by his fear, voices a simplified version of his culture's values, the latter voices its doubts. Obierika briefly but significantly questions general practices such as the discarding of twins and Okonkwo's participation in the execution of Ikemefuna, and at the end of the novel he is left contemplating the transition of Okonkwo from hero to pariah. Similarly Nwoye's apostasy opens up another horizon: by espousing the new chirographic culture he creates the potential for one of his descendants to write a novel like *Things Fall Apart*.

Achebe's first novel, then, can be seen as a unique totalizing and syncretic achievement. Its totalizing ability is most clearly visible in its syncretism. While rescuing oral cultures from their inevitable transitoriness, writing also alienates the objects as well as the unreflexive (or rather less reflexive) subject of that world by allowing one to examine them at a distance. In turn the fixity, distance, and scrutiny permitted by writing facilitate greater familiarity with and understanding of self and the world. This dialectic of distance and proximity, of alienation and understanding is inevitably involved in the configuration of Achebe's novel. *Things Fall Apart* documents, among other things, the destruction of oral culture by a chirographic one. However, Achebe uses that very process of chirographic documentation in order to recreate and preserve a symbolic version of the destroyed culture; in recording the oral culture's preoccupation with the present, Achebe historicizes its evanescence. The novel incorporates its own condition and occasion into itself. However, the most fascinating aspect of this totalization is that while *Things Fall Apart* depicts the mutual misunderstanding and antagonism of the colonizing and colonized worlds, the very process of this depiction, in its capacity as a *written oral* narrative, transcends the Manichean relations by a brilliant synthesis of oral and chirographic cultures. By deliberately adhering to a flat surface Achebe obtains a result curiously similar to the effect obtained by one of Picasso's paintings: the illusion of depth and perspective, of the third dimension in symbolic representation, is deliberately wrenched and displaced in order to create a two-dimensional representation that includes within it an abstract reminder about the third dimension. While Picasso drew his inspiration from West African art, Achebe draws his from West European fiction. Like Picasso's paintings, Achebe's novel presents us with sophisticated primitivism, with a deliberate return to an innocence re-presented.

IV

The syncretism of Achebe's fiction, most clearly evident in *Things Fall Apart* and *Arrow of God*, has two important ideological consequences. As we saw at the beginning of this essay, the Third World writer uses European languages because of certain ideological and technological pressures. In Achebe's case there is an additional compulsion to write about his culture in English because not to do so would leave the definition and representation of his society at the mercy of (usually) racist colonial writers. However, under these constraints he uses English in a way that deterritorializes it. By deliberately simplifying and willing a certain kind of poverty he pushes the English language to its limits: the rhythm of the endless paratactic sentences negates the diversity and complexity of which the language is capable. The deliberate simplicity is combined with a dryness and sobriety of voice to create a new register. Achebe develops a mythic voice that can evoke sympathy and concern while remaining entirely neutral. This neutral, mythic voice, which is entirely new in modern English literature, is able to recuperate a vanishing cultural experience without lapsing into sentimentality or spitefulness. In addition to this innovative deterritorialization, Achebe is able to expand the English language through the transfusion of Igbo material. For example, the transliterated proverbs reintroduce into the language a kind of figurative, analogical element that has gradually been displaced by the scientific-empiric consciousness that favours precision based on literalness. Finally, as we have seen, Achebe also expands the form of the novel through his sophisticated primitivism. Thus we must conclude that *Things Fall Apart* is able to do justice to the phenomenology of oral cultures and that by deterritorializing the English language and the novelistic form, Achebe's novel also contributes to the negative dialogic relations between African and English literatures. Achebe takes the English language and the novelistic form and creates a unique African form with them. Of course, this does not mean that African fiction cannot be written in African languages, but it also does not mean that English can be excluded as a language of African fiction on purely ideological grounds.

The second ideological implication of the syncretism is a less happy one. Both the synthesis of oral and chirographic cultures enacted by the form of *Things Fall Apart* and its deterritorialization of English contradict the substance of the novel and thereby reveal the major ideological implication embedded in the contradiction. The content creates a longing for a vanished herioc culture, but the linguistic and cultural syntheses within the form of the novel point to future syncretic possibilities. While the content laments a loss and points an accusing finger at colonialist destruction, the form glories in the pleasures of a new formal synthesis and transcends the Manichean antagonisms of the colonizer and the colonized. Thus while the initial layer of the emotive intentionality coincides with the traditional ideology of colonized resentment and bitterness and reveals the ideological bondage of the colonized man who is caught between historical catalepsy and cultural petrification,[15] the deeper layer of emotive intentionality which finds pleasure in linguistic and formal syncretism implies a freedom from that ideological double-bind. Achebe's long silence in the field of fiction is probably due to his preoccupation with catalepsy and petrification and perhaps to the ideological pressure to discard the use of English as creative medium.

Notes

[1] I have examined the social, political, and ideological dimensions of this dialogue in detail elsewhere. See *Manichean Aesthetics: The Politics of Literature in Colonial Africa* (Amherst, Massachusetts: University of Massachusetts Press, 1983).

[2] Jack Goody, *The Domestication of the Savage Mind* (Cambridge: Cambridge University Press, 1977) and Walter J. Ong, *Orality and Literacy: The Technologizing of the Word* (London: Methuen, 1982). For a very useful descriptive survey of the work being done on orality and literacy see F. Niyi Akinnaso, "On the Differences Between Spoken and Written Language," *Language and Speech* 25, 2 (1982), 97-125.

[3] Goody, p. 43.

[4] Goody, p. 44.

[5] Ernst Cassirer, *The Philosophy of Symbolic Form*, Vol. 2 *Mythical Thought* (New Haven: Yale University Press, 1955).

[6] E. H. Cooley, quoted in Goody, p. 15.

[7] M. M. Ngal, "Literary Creation and Oral Civilization," *New Literary History* VIII, 3 (Spring 1977), 337-338.

[8] Harold Scheub, "Body and Image in Oral Narrative Performance," *New Literary History* VIII, 3 (Spring 1977), 346-348.

[9] Ngal, pp. 341-343.

[10] Ruth Finnegan, *Oral Literature in Africa* (Oxford: Clarendon Press, 1970).

[11] Chinua Achebe, *Things Fall Apart* (Greenwich, Connecticut: Fawcett Publications, 1959), p. 7. All further references to this novel will be incorporated in the essay.

[12] Achebe feels that a "new English" will have to be "still in full communion with its ancestral home but altered to suit its new African surroundings." For his discussion of this topic see "The English Language and the African Writer," *Transition* 4, 18 (1965), 27-30.

[13] The predominance of the "background" characterizes the entire novel. As Robert M. Wren points out, "In page count, the marriage group (wedding and family chapters together) take up more than one-fourth of the novel, and in them there is virtually no plot progression whatever. The chapters on the agricultural year, including the account of Okonkwo's disastrous beginnings as a farmer, amount to one fifth of the novel. The white man and his religion are dominant in about one-third of the novel—almost all of Parts Two and Three. Through most of the novel Okonkwo is passive or subordinate, though he is the link that holds all together." *Achebe's World* (Washington, D.C.: Three Continents Press, 1980), p. 25.

[14] M. M. Bakhtin, *The Dialogic Imagination: Four Essays* (Austin, Texas: University of Texas Press, 1981), p. 37.

[15] I have explored this dilemma in detail elsewhere. See *Manichean Aesthetics*, pp. 178-184.

Okonkwo's Walk: The Choreography of Things Falling Apart

Russell McDougall

—People are art in Africa. Icon and act stem from common roots.[1]

The impulse of my re-consideration of Chinua Achebe's novel *Things Fall Apart* comes, as my epigraph implies, from Robert Farris Thompson's readings in African art history. I am indebted particularly to his discussion of sculpture in the context of music and motion, where the iconography of posture is revealed as encoding the principles of a cultural aesthetic. While Thompson's own concerns are not of a literary nature, a major review of his seminal work, re-issued in 1979 and entitled *African Art in Motion: Icon and Act*, concluded that one aspect of the book's importance is in providing a whole range of concepts derived from iconology that might be useful in studying artistic traditions other than the visual.[2] Considering these concepts in terms of literary criticism may open up new possibilities for inter-cultural dialogue (*inter*-pretation). This article is a small part of a much larger study: it marks my first tentative steps into a wide-ranging exploration of the kinetics of African literature.

The structures of significance that Chinua Achebe's novel posits in terms of the gestures and attitudes of the body inevitably derive from the cultural codes of physical behaviour, as they must in the literature of any people. In Africa, however, the same aesthetic criteria that govern the production of art, traditionally at least, are brought to bear in the organization of these cultural codes (glibly referred to in Western marketing psychology as "body language"). Non-verbal modes of discourse are more central to African cultures than they have become in the Gutenberg Galaxy of the Western world. In traditional Africa, as Thompson argues: "The road to social purification and destiny is predicated upon a process through which the person takes on the essential attributes of aesthetically defined perfection in order to live in visible proximity to the divine" (p. 1). The implication for the verbal act is that it remains what Kenneth Burke preferentially calls "the dancing of an attitude," much more inherently gestural than is the case in highly industrialized cultures, where it conforms with the general "sedentary trend from the bodily to the abstract."[3]

For the purpose of characterization, motion is stylized in *Things Fall Apart*, absorbing the individual into a moral universe explored in the novel through gesture and posture that are imbued with iconic significance. Okonkwo's road to social contamination is charted by the "language" inherent in the attitudes of his body, which characterizes him as aesthetically imperfect and spiritually retarded. The image of him dangling at the end of a rope from a tree at the conclusion of the novel is linked inevitably with what we are told in the very early stages of the first chapter about his way of walking, heels hardly touching the ground, as if on springs.

This paper proceeds in three phases. The first focus is upon Okonkwo's gait. As the point around which the novel's "widening gyre" turns, it offers an aptly moving image for the centre that cannot hold. Second, moving towards a generalization about the kinetic mode of other fiction, a few other examples of significant movement are given. And finally, not to give too much away too early, my conclusion bears some ironic relation to the macabre cliché exploited by Fielding at the end of *Jonathan Wild*, where the hero, asked if he is afraid to hang, answers: "D--n me, it is only a dance without music."

Okonkwo's destiny is to commit "an offense against the Earth" by taking his own life.[4] There are two reasons for this. One is stated emotionally by his friend Obierika in the final stages of the novel, and will be given "a reasonable paragraph" (p. 191) in the book the Commissioner intends to write under the title of "The Pacification of the Primitive Tribes of the Lower Niger"—that is, he is driven to kill himself by the white man's tactics of immobilizing vital tradition and fragmenting tribal society. Potentially offering the most serious opposition to these tactics, Okonkwo becomes the tragic symbol of their success. But

Things Fall Apart defines itself against the Commissioner's book, as an account of colonial history from the point of view of the colonized rather than that of the colonizer and so from the perspective of African ontology instead of Eurocentric historiography. This is the context for the other motive behind Okonkwo's fate, his lack of personal balance.

Certainly in what follows I am not the first to see the tragedy of Okonkwo in terms of his failure to balance the male and female constituents of personality (nor to notice the importance of the female principle in the design of the novel).[5] But the relation of this generally to an African aesthetic of moderation and mediation, and more specifically to normative stability of stance and other forms of equipoise alluded to within the novel, seems to have gone unnoticed. We might expect a man famed for his expertise in the "wrestling dance" (p. 43), in which one of the central principles of success is never to be caught off balance, would not lack personal equilibrium. But Okonkwo is dominated by fear of failure and weakness, by "the fear of himself, lest he should be found to resemble his father." We are told that he is "ruled by one passion—to hate everything his father Unoka had loved" (p. 17). Unoka was very good on the flute and "his happiest moments were the two or three moons after the harvest when the village musicians brought down their instruments, hung above the fireplace" (p. 8). But he is lazy and so is known as *agbala*, which not only means a man who has taken no title but also is "another name for a woman" (p. 17). Unoka allows aesthetic considerations to outweigh practical interests, and so does not particularly associate the rhythm of the seasons with the rhythm of planting, propagation and harvesting. Overreacting to his father's faults, Okonkwo denies himself the internal symmetry on which a person's moral well-being must traditionally be based, a symmetry that is properly expressed in the attitudes of the body and in the phrasing of physical movement. He takes a purely utilitarian view of life, shutting out all aesthetic pleasures and opening the door to suffering: "During the planting season Okonkwo worked daily on his farms from cock-crow until the chickens went to roost. He was a very strong man and rarely felt fatigue. But his wives and young children were not as strong, and so they suffered" (p. 17). In reaction against his *agbala* father, he shuts out the music inherent in the cosmic rhythms on which he depends for his livelihood; and he allows the male principle to dominate his life. But Agbala is also Oracle of the Hills and Caves, spokesman for the all-powerful earth goddess, and when Okonkwo cuts himself off from the female principle he denies himself the essential spiritual relationship with the earth, pre-determining the final act of suicide that is an offense against it.

There is a pattern of inevitability running through the novel, a rhythm to its design. It has been described as a pattern of tragedy organized by the integration of ironies.[6] For my purpose, however, the tension and stress should be seen as stemming from polymetric principles of rhythm and contrast, embodying a cultural style that is common to much of Africa. The main points can be summarized briefly. And it should be noted that the dramatic action here outlined encompasses the three major themes of Igbo masquerade drama: the tension between men and women, between age and youth, and between personal competitiveness and community harmony.[7] In compensation for the murder of one of its daughters, Umuofia demands from the neighbouring village of Mbaino a young man and a virgin, according to a rule of symmetry which generalizes the two chosen and so puts justice on the social rather than the individual plane. Okonkwo is asked to receive the boy into his household until the clan decides his fate. Three years later the Oracle of Agbala decrees the boy's death and the oldest man in the village, "a great and fearless warrior in his time" (p. 55), advises Okonkwo not to have a hand in the killing because the boy now calls him father. But out of his own instability, the fear of seeming weak and effeminate, he disregards the advice and cuts the boy down with his machete. Before this he insists that Ezinma, his favorite child, behave according to her sex; afterwards he begins to wish that she were a boy. In doing so he risks offending the earth goddess by refusing to acknowledge the female principle of life which is associated with aesthetic beauty and with the mother of the earth. (In Okonkwo's own motherland, Ezinma is called Crystal of Beauty, as her mother had been called in her youth. The priestess not only calls Ezinma her own daughter but also the daughter of Agbala, a masculine god who is nevertheless the voice of the Supreme Mother, the earth goddess. By this spiritual parentage and by the nomenclatory image of crystal, we are again reminded in a human context which is defined both aesthetically and religiously, of the importance of balance and symmetry.) Later, the priestess visits Okonkwo, saying that Agbala desires to see his daughter. By allowing his wife to follow the priestess, Okonkwo is himself led into defiance of the god, for he goes after her to the sacred cave. It is clear at the end of the novel that the curse the priestess puts upon her tracker, although seeming to apply at the time to his wife, in fact anticipates Okonkwo's death. "'Somebody is walking behind me!' she screams. 'May he [Agbala] twist your neck until you see your heels'" (p. 99). The next major event in the pattern tracing Okonkwo's destiny to offend the earth is when he commits the crime of killing a clansman, his gun accidentally exploding. Since it is inadvertent, the crime is classified as female. His punishment, then, is exile for seven years, and so he flees to his motherland. But, rather than regarding it as a place of refuge and renewal, he succumbs to despair, forgetting that "Mother is supreme" and so risking offense to the ancestral spirits of his mother's people by identifying their homeland as his punishment. He finally returns to the land of his father, where he murders the Commissioner's messenger and then, realizing that Umuofia will not support his untempered masculine action by declaring war, he commits suicide. Thus he follows his father, who "died of the swelling which was an abomination to the earth goddess" (p. 21). But suicide is a masculine form of "offense against the Earth," completely willful, an act of unbalanced individualism.

This whole movement towards suicide, in terms of spiritual alienation from the earth and the mother, through fear of the female principle in the self and subsequent overemphasis of masculinity, is summed up at the beginning by Okonkwo's way of walking: "his heels hardly touched the ground and he seemed to walk on springs, as if he was going to pounce on somebody" (p. 8). The image is of a man aggressive and unbalanced by his defiance of gravity, which represents a denial of the earth. I am reminded of the symbolism of those "skyward-facing" masks in Igbo masquerades which are worn horizontally on top of the head and combine human and animal features to represent male energy and repression: "These depict fierce ghosts of men who in life were lawbreakers or otherwise harmful. They do not dance but like other distorted masks run through the village arousing fear and excitement by threatening violence and disorder."[8] The normative stability of stance cannot be stressed strongly enough in relation to its impact on spiritual and social well-being. In fact, the iconic significance of Okonkwo's style of walking in defiance of gravity is not only an implicit denial of the power of the earth mother, but also, more generally, an un-conscious rejection of the West African way of cultivating divin-ity "through richly stabilized traditions of personal balance" (*African Art in Motion*, p. 24).

This is borne out by Okonkwo's inadvertently influencing his son, Nwoye, to embrace Christianity. Because Okonkwo is alienated from the poetry inherent in nature's rhythms he re-presses his son's love of the mythic element in his mother's tales, forcing "masculine stories of violence and bloodshed" (p. 52) upon him instead. Hence he starves the boy's spirit and erodes his faith until finally, with tragic irony (since the tradi-tional approach to the divine, as I have said already, is an aes-thetic one), Nwoye is drawn to Christianity by its poetry:

> It was not the mad logic of the Trinity that captivated
> him. He did not understand it. It was the poetry of the
> new religion, something felt in the marrow. . . . He felt
> a relief within as the hymn poured into his parched
> soul. The words of the hymn were like the drops of
> frozen rain melting on the dry palate of the panting
> earth.   (p. 137)

But this imagery connecting Christianity with the rejuvenation of the living earth is ironic also, since the new god, as the mis-sionaries make quite plain, has nothing to do with the tradi-tional ones and therefore in fact opposes the supremacy of the earth mother.

Okonkwo can be seen as the type of destructive power, the embodiment of a kind of death wish. The physical attitudes he assumes, rather than functioning traditionally "to restore an-cient modes of self-presentation in contexts of important indica-tion" (*African Art in Motion*, p. xii), express power without dig-nity and an absence of humour that anticipates suffering. He is, then, the anti-type of the life force, of the true power of incarna-tion. And the context of indication here is his ushering in, iron-ically, the era of a new god.

For Okonkwo's way of walking can be seen not only as an image in opposition to the aesthetic and spiritual tradition of personal balance but also, more precisely, as an image anticipat-ing Christianity, which similarly defies the attraction of the earth, shifting the focus of spiritual idealism away farm the ma-terial world. Erwin Panofsky has shown, for instance, that:

> This ascent from the material to the immaterial world
> is what the Pseudo-Areopagite and John the Scot de-
> scribe—in contrast to the customary use of this term—as

> the 'anagogical approach' (*anagogicus mos*, literally
> translated: 'the upward-leading method'); and this is
> what Suger [the Abbot whose rebuilding the Church of
> Saint-Denis pinpoints the origin of the Gothic archi-
> tectural style] professed as a theologian, proclaimed as
> a poet, and practised as a patron of the arts and an ar-
> ranger of liturgical spectacles.[9]

Functioning in terms of a fundamental African principle, that
action is a mode of thought (*African Art in Motion*, p. 117),
Okonkwo's unbalanced and "anagogical" style of movement
ironically calls forth (in a structural sense) Christianity.

Okonkwo's walk is not an isolated instance of significant
movement; it sets in motion a whole chain of kinetic images
propelled towards his dancing at the end of a rope. Wole
Soyinka argues that: "tragedy through action" is at the centre of
Achebe's novel, defining action as "a movement within the image . . . not merely a crescendo of passions."[10] The iconography
of posture and gesture throughout *Things Fall Apart* identifies
the novel as grounded in traditional aesthetics even as it charts
the decline of their significance in the spiritual context of the
community. Two other brief examples must suffice to confirm
the truth of this statement; I leave its political implication for
my conclusion. The first example refers to "the theme of head
portage [which] occurs with formalized repetition in the arts of
Africa" (*African Art in Motion*, p. 96) and has its roots in the oc-
cupational patterns of the traditional life of the people:

> The fact was the Obiageli had been making *inyanga*
> with her pot. She had balanced it on her head, folded
> her arms in front of her and began to sway her waist
> like a grown-up young lady. When the pot fell down
> and broke she burst out laughing. She only began to
> weep when they got near the iroko tree outside their
> compound.   (p. 44)

Here it should be realized that balancing an object on the head
without supporting it with the hands is not simply a phe-
nomenon of superior poise. In adulthood, for instance, it may
represent "attainment of transcendental equilibrium . . . en-
abling a person to communicate mind itself by the quality of his
composure" (*African Art in Motion*, p. 96). Hence the act of balancing extends the notion of personal stability in relation to the
earth resulting in a walk in which, as Peggy Harper says, "the
modulations of the ground surface are taken up in the flexibility
of the hips and knees."[11] Achebe relies upon this iconic signifi-

cance of the act of balancing to communicate the child's ignorance and instability as an omen of a more profound loss of balance in society. The prophetic nature of the child's inflexibility
of movement and of the lack of mental calm it mirrors relates to
my final example of the iconic mode of the danced art of *Things
Fall Apart*, so that I may cite it here without further comment.
Enoch, whose devotion to the new faith seems to exceed even
the white man's, to such an extent that, although he is the son of
the snake-priest, he is believed to have killed and eaten the sacred python, "always seemed in great haste . . . and when he
stood or walked his heels came together and his feet opened
outwards as if the had quarreled and meant to go in different di-
rections" (p. 170).

The gestural nature of *Things Fall Apart* adumbrates the
aesthetic relationship that exists between African literature and
dance. According to an art history beginning only now to be
written in its own terms, the icons of African art are traditionally
"more influenced by the vital body in implied motion, by forms
of flexibility, than by realism of anatomy *per se*" (*African Art in
Motion*, p. xiv). The "active potentiality" of the image in the
plastic arts of traditional African cultures (p. xii), the manner in
which motifs of stillness are underlined by motion, has been
convincingly demonstrated by Thompson in the context of
dance. Although the novel in particular is an imported form, as
is the English language in which it is often written, the traditional aesthetics of movement provide a basis for the literary arts
of Africa which often leads to a subtle transformation of the foreign model (which evolved in late seventeenth and early eigh-
teenth-century England from completely different criteria of
taste, judgment and belief). Hence an understanding of the kinetic principles of African dance as the matrix from which general cultural principles of balance and flexibility evolve will
extend the impact of the literary work. I can extend what I have
already said of Okonkwo's walk, for example, by placing it in the
following context.

Recalling Panofsky's discussion of "the upward-leading
method" of Gothic cathedral architecture, Thompson observes
that the desire of the ballet dancer to soar through the air in a
sense mirrors the architects' search for God "through 'anagogic'
filials, pointed towards heaven." When Western dance traditions cultivate a preference for what he calls "asymmetrical posture or stylized instability," airborne displays of agility in African

dance, if they do occur, are ultimately to confirm the role of gravity and to stress the importance of personal balance (*African Art in Motion*, pp. 24-25). Thus, Achebe writes in "Beware, Soul Brother":

> Our ancestors, soul brother, were wiser
> than is often made out. Remember
> they gave Ala, great goddess
> of their earth, sovereignty too over
> their arts for they understood
> too well those hard-headed
> men of departed dance where a man's
> foot must return whatever beauties
> it may weave in the air, where
> it must return for safety
> and renewal of strength. Take care
> then, mother's son, lest you become
> a dancer disinherited in mid-dance
> hanging a lame foot in air like the hen
> in a strange unfamiliar compound. . . .

Here the lame dancer is an image of disinheritance of the earth and a warning against allowing traditional values to be displaced by Christianity:

> . . . beware soul brother
> of the lures of ascension day
> the day of soporific levitation
> on high winds of skysong. . . .[12]

Within the context of traditional aesthetic and spiritual principles, where "icon defines itself in act" (*African Art in Motion*, p. 117), Okonkwo's unbalanced and "anagogical" gait designates conceptually a departure from the ideal human image which dominates African art and dance, an image rising from "feet set flat and firm upon the earth" (p. 24). We are told there is a saying in Umuofia "that as a man danced so the drums were beaten for him" (p. 170); and I have said already that the kinetic image of Okonkwo actually initiates the structure of events which will bring forth Christianity. That image, we now see, is the one that is central to the dance in Eastern culture, of the individual upon his toes, which Achebe glosses in African perspective: "as if he were about to pounce on somebody." The active potential of the image, then, is to remind us of the hypocrisy of the religious thrust towards the immaterial, as Achebe tells his soul brother when he warns him against the lures of the sky in ascension day:

> . . . beware
> for others there will be that day
> lying in wait leaden-footed, tone-dead
> passionate only for the deep entrails
> of our soul. . . .

Against my argument it might be said that in much of urban Africa dance has lost its key position in society (though on the whole this is not the impression that the fiction gives—John Munonye's *A Dancer of Fortune*, for instance). The transformation of society has meant the modification or even the disappearance of the functions traditionally performed by dance. But it is too easy to generalize about urban dance as so many degenerate forms stripped of all inherent value. Judith Lynne Hanna has shown, for instance, that although Africa has been profoundly affected by urbanization and technological development, the basic contributions of dance to society continue, adapting form to new behaviour.[13] It is not entirely ironic, then, in Achebe's second novel, *No Longer at Ease*, that Obi is told when he arrives in Lagos, from the country: "Dancing is very important nowadays."[14] In this novel, however, Western influenced styles, characterized by ballroom positioning and lack of "real" movement, are associated with a theme of moral corruption. The culminating development of this theme is in fact presented as a dance sequence, with Obi "leading" a schoolgirl (who has come to seek his help in obtaining a scholarship) into his bedroom:

> 'You dance very well,' he whispered as she pressed herself against him, breathing very fast and hard. He put her arms round his neck and brought her lips within a centimeter of his. They no longer paid any attention to the beat of the high-life. Obi steered her towards his bedroom. She made a half-hearted show of resisting, then followed.   (p. 157)

Dancing without regard to rhythm, Obi's absence of "real" movement here is indicative of the nature of his tragedy, not through action, as in *Things Fall Apart*, but through the lack of it. Soyinka makes a similar point about the third novel, *Arrow of God*; but I am already beyond the scope of my argument. How does Obi's dance relate to Okonkwo's walk? The elders of the village answer this in a nutshell. When Obi returns from his studies in England he is perceived as one who has been "wrestling in the spirit world," and one of his kinsmen observes: "he is Ogbuefi Okonkwo come back" (pp. 54, 56). In the approx-

imation of Okonkwo's gait to Western dance modes there is an
anticipation of Obi's dancing the high-life as if it were a form of
low life. Okot p'Bitek's *Song of Lawino* express the kinetic relationship quite explicitly:

> Dancing without a song
> Dancing silently like wizards.
> If someone tries
> To force me to dance this dance
> I feel like hanging myself
> Feet first.[15]

Achebe speaks of his aim as "education, in the best sense
of the word," meaning that it does not involve the rejection of
values alien to indigenous thought:

> I think perhaps that this is a reflection of the funda-
> mental Ibo attitude to change. The fanatic was the ex-
> ception rather than the rule. Because the Ibo have
> very strong belief in dualities: things do not come
> singly, but in twos. That's very, very important in ev-
> erything we do. So that if there's one form of religion,
> there is bound to be another form.[16]

The poet from whom, of course, Achebe takes the novel's title
poses the unanswerable question: "How can we know the dancer
from the dance?" In the end, we cannot distinguish Okonkwo's
unbalanced rejection of Christianity from the missionaries' introduction of "the idea of a single-minded dogmatic belief."[17]
Achebe's canon has the power of myth, and in this Okonkwo is
seminal: bearing a hand in the sacrifice of a boy who calls one
father is moving in a way that defines Christianity.

Edwin Denby's conceptualization of dance is useful to interpret the rhythmic structure of history, its active potentiality as
myth. "In dancing," Denby says, "one keeps taking a step and re-
covering one's balance. The risk is part of the rhythm."[18] In the
novel, "things fall apart" when Okonkwo violates the communal ideals of personal balance. But Achebe's concern ultimately
is with restoring the balance: "You have all heard of the African
Personality: of African democracy, of the African way to social-
ism, of negritude, and so on. They are all props we have fashioned at different times to help us get on our feet again. Once we
are up we shan't need any of them any more."[19] This was the
animating principle of his fiction: to get "Africa" back on its feet,
to restore that sense of balance which is so central to the micro-
cosm of the dominant art of dance. Writing becomes verbal
choreography of movement through time. The rediscovery of

history, the past that lives in the present through the ancestral medium of dance, reveals the dynamics of change and so perhaps enables a more considered or consciously directed movement into the future. In this way aesthetic principles are translated into political doctrine, as is the case traditionally when the solo dancer steps into the communal ring—where creativity is void unless actively sanctioned by the chorus, where performance embodies the person of moral perfection rather than the individual performer, where identity is symbolically rediscovered and confirmed through social interaction. Achebe's writing declares an attitude to history, as choreography; but he stops short of prophecy, for once the rhythmic pattern of the past has been established the future becomes a matter of balancing the beat with progressive improvisations, crossing memory with active imagination

> remember also your children
> for they in their time will want
> a place for their feet when
> they come of age and the dance
> of the future is born
> for them.

("Beware, Soul Brother")

Notes

[1] Robert Farris Thompson, *African Art in Motion: Icon and Act* (1974; rpt. Los Angeles: University of California Press, 1979), p. 112. Further references are incorporated in the text.

[2] Robert G. Armstrong, rev. of *African Art in Motion*, *Research in African Literatures* 12 (1981), 535.

[3] Kenneth Burke, *The Philosophy of Literary Form: Studies in Symbolic Action* (Baton Rouge: Louisiana State University Press, 1941), p. 16.

[4] *Things Fall Apart* (1959; rpt. New York: Fawcett Crest, 1969), p. 190. Further references are incorporated in the text.

[5] See, for example, G. D. Killam, *The Novels of Chinua Achebe* (London: Heinemann Educational, 1969), p. 20 ff.; and Donald G. Ackley, "The Male-Female Motif in *Things Fall Apart*," *Studies in Black Literature* 5, 1 (1974), 1-6.

[6] Killam, p. 33.

[7] Monni Adams, *Designs for Living: Symbolic Communication in African Art* (Cambridge, Massachusetts: Carpenter Center for the Visual Arts, Harvard University, 1982), p. 73.

[8] Adams, p. 74.

[9] Erwin Panofsky, *Meaning in the Visual Arts* (Garden City, New York: Doubleday, 1955), p. 128.

[10] Wole Soyinka, "And After the Narcissist?" *African Forum* 1, 1 (1966), 63.

[11] Peggy Harper, "Dance in Nigeria," *Ethnomusicology* 13, 1 (1969), 288.

[12] "Beware, Soul Brother," in the verse collection of the same title (London: Heinemann Educational, 1979), pp. 29-30. Further references are incorporated in the text.

[13] Judith Lynne Hanna, "African Dance: The Continuity of Change," *Yearbook of the International Folk Music Council* 5 (1973).

[14] *No Longer at Ease* (1960; rpt. New York: Fawcett Premier, 1969), p. 21. Further references are incorporated in the text.

[15] Okot p'Bitek, *Song of Lawino: An African Lament* (1966; rpt. Nairobi: East African Publishing House, 1972), p. 41.

[16] Interview in *Times Literary Supplement*, 26 February 1982, p. 209.

[17] Interview, p. 209.

[18] Edwin Denby, "Forms in Motion and in Thought, " in *Dances, Buildings and People in the Streets* (New York: Horizon, 1965), p. 165.

[19] "The Novelist as Teacher," in *Morning Yet on Creation Day* (Garden City, New York: Anchor/Doubleday, 1975), p. 71.

Eternal Sacred Order versus Conventional Wisdom: A Consideration of Moral Culpability in the Killing of Ikemefuna in *Things Fall Apart*

Damian U. Opata

> As the man who had cleared his throat drew up and raised his matchet, Okonkwo looked away. He heard the blow. The pot fell and broke in the sand. He heard Ikemefuna cry, 'My father, they have killed me!' as he ran towards him. Dazed with fear, Okonkwo drew his matchet and cut him down. He was afraid of being thought weak. (*Things Fall Apart*, p. 43)

Okonkwo's killing of Ikemefuna—his knottiest moral dilemma in the novel—has generally been seen by critics as an unconscionable act that is tantamount to an offense against the gods of the land. After Ikemefuna's death, Okonkwo's closest friend, Obierika, tells him that what he did "will not please the Earth" because "it is the kind of action for which the goddess wipes out whole families" (p. 46). Earlier, Ezeudu, "the oldest man" in Okonkwo's own quarter of Umuofia, had told Okonkwo not to have anything to do with the killing of Ikemefuna. He said, "That boy calls you father. Do not bear a hand in his death" (p. 40). The authorial voice which follows after the killing of Ikemefuna ascribes a psychological motive of fear to Okonkwo's actions.

Following these trips from the text, many critics have been unequivocal in alleging that Okonkwo committed an offense by having a hand in the killing of Ikemefuna. David Carroll (1970, p. 44; 1980, pp. 42-43), Charles Nnolim (p. 58), Oladele Taiwo (p. 118), G. D. Killam (p. 20), and Robert M. Wren (p. 44) share this view that Okonkwo committed an offense by taking part in the killing of Ikemefuna. Solomon Iyasere (p. 102) sympathizes with Okonkwo for the humane qualities that he showed by looking away as Ikemefuna was about to be killed, but Iyasere neither exonerates Okonkwo nor holds him culpable for the death of Ikemefuna. From the available critical literature I have examined regarding Okonkwo's role in the killing Ikemefuna, no critic has seen fit to exonerate Okonkwo for killing Ikemefuna. The attempt of this paper shall be to establish that, although Okonkwo felt some temporal sense of moral revulsion after he had killed Ikemefuna, he cannot thereby be said to have committed any offense against Earth. This defense of Okonkwo shall be looked at from two levels: from internal evidence in *Things Fall Apart* and from what critics have made of some of the evidence available in the text.

Ikemefuna—a sacrificial lamb—is first introduced to us as "a doomed lad," "an ill-fated lad" (p. 6). The young virgin, with whom he is brought to Umuofia [as appeasement from the people of Mbaino who had killed a daughter of Umuofia] is not even mentioned by name. All we are told about her is that she belongs to Ogbuefi Udo, the man whose wife was murdered by the people of Mbaino. Ikemefuna, on the other hand, is a communal property, but Okonkwo is asked to look after him as "there was no hurry to decide his fate" (p. 9). Because he was regarded as a sacrificial lamb, Ikemefuna's death was already a *fait accompli*, at least in the eyes of Mbaino people. Under Okonkwo's roof, Ikemefuna is treated as any other member of Okonkwo's family, and he soon starts to address Okonkwo as his father. Had Okonkwo not extended the same fatherly love he has for all his children to Ikemefuna, but treated him as a captive and an object of sacrifice—which he actually was—he would probably not have endeared himself to Okonkwo to the extent of calling him "Father." Indeed, if he lost memories of his own home, it was because of the humane way in which he was integrated into Okonkwo's household. But at the end of three years, the people of Umuofia decided to kill him. As Ogbuefi Ezeudu says:

> Yes, Umuofia has decided to kill him. The Oracle of
> the Hills and the Caves has pronounced it. They will
> take him outside Umuofia as is the custom, and kill
> him there. But I want [you] to have nothing to do with
> it. He calls you father.   (p. 40)

Ogbuefi Ezeudu's warning is significant because he is the oldest man in Okonkwo's quarter of Umuofia, and he is, by tradition, a representative of the collective spiritual conscience of the people as well as a mediator between the living and the dead. His advice should be seen as authoritative and well-intentioned. His injunction is, on a general plane, premised on the conventional wisdom that a man should not kill another who is his father, or who calls him father. Here, conventional wisdom is in agreement with the traditional sacred order. All this is well under normal circumstances. In the case under consideration, Umuofia is asked to carry out a divine command. We are not told much about the people whose function it is to carry out this type of command, but from the description on page 40 ("a group of elders from all the nine villages of Umuofia") and from the reference to this group on page 41 ("The next day, the men returned with a pot of wine"), we may conclude that it is the duty of the elders. Earlier we had been told that because of Okonkwo's personal achievements, he had already joined the group of elders (p. 6). If Ikemefuna had been kept in a household other than Okonkwo's, Okonkwo would probably have been one of the elders to go to that household to convey the decision of Umuofia to kill Ikemefuna in accordance with the wish of the Oracle of the Hills and the Caves.

What options were open to Okonkwo after Ezeudu had spoken to him? Is it possible for us to find out his reaction to Ezeudu's warning? We shall take the latter question first. Ezeudu's advice is delivered like a command: "That boy calls you father. Do not bear a hand in his death"; later on, the warning is restated thus: "I want [you] to have nothing to do with it. He calls you father." Okonkwo's opinion is not sought; he is given an injunction. Since Ezeudu is the oldest man in Okonkwo's own quarter of Umuofia, he can be seen as the direct representative of the ancestors of that particular quarter. His words, therefore, have the force of law. Because Okonkwo did not protest or even argue with Ezeudu, we may feel safe to assume that he accepted Ezeudu's advice. This assumption is borne out later in the novel. When the people set out to kill Ikemefuna, Okonkwo was walking directly behind him (p. 42), but by the time they arrived at the outskirts of Umuofia, where Ikemefuna would be killed, Okonkwo had withdrawn to the rear. The passage reads:

> One of the men behind him cleared his throat. Ikeme-
> funa looked back, and the man growled at him to go on
> and not stand looking back. The way he said it sent
> cold fear down Ikemefuna's back. His hands trembled
> vaguely on the black pot he carried. Why had

> Okonkwo withdrawn to the rear? Ikemefuna felt his
> legs melting under him. And he was afraid to look
> back.   (p. 43)

What is the proper interpretation of Okonkwo's decision to
withdraw to the rear? It is plausible to believe that he did so in
order not to "bear a hand in the death" of Ikemefuna (p. 40). His
decision to withdraw to the back can be seen as willingness on
his part to listen to the advice of Ezeudu. If we also add to this
the fact that he "looked away" when the man who had earlier
growled "drew up" to kill Ikemefuna (p. 43), we can say that
Okonkwo neither wanted to "bear a hand" in Ikemefuna's death
nor see him cut down (p. 43). It may be that Okonkwo would
have taken this decision if Ezeudu had not spoken to him, but
since he did, we can assume that it was a way of reacting posi-
tively to Ezeudu's advice.

We now return to the first question: What were the options open to Okonkwo when Ezeudu came to warn him that he
should have nothing to do with the killing to Ikemefuna? We
shall consider the choice open to Okonkwo at two levels. When
"the men returned" the following day to take Ikemefuna to the
place where he would be killed (p. 41), what were the things he
could have elected to do? He could have chosen to do one of
two things: either accompany the elders or stay behind. The latter will eventually turn out to be Obierika's counsel. Okonkwo,
however, did not stay behind. Are we then to condemn him for
not staying behind? Before we answer yes or no to this question,
we should be reminded that Okonkwo is one of the elders of
Umuofia. It was the elders who came to convey the message of
the decision of Umuofia to kill Ikemefuna. The same group of
elders returned the following day to take Ikemefuna away. It is
possible that one of Okonkwo's reasons for deciding to accompany them is that he is one of them. But there is a more important reason: it might have simply been a question of strategy. After Okonkwo had been informed of the decision to kill Ikemefuna, he had told Ikemefuna that he was to be taken home the
following day. After all, even pious Abraham in a somewhat related situation had to pretend to Isaac. Moreover, Okonkwo is
the person who went to Mbaino "as the proud and imperious
emissary of war" (p. 9) to ask for "a young man and a virgin as
compensation" (p. 8) for the murder of Ogbuefi Udo's wife. In
addition, Okonkwo had acted as guardian and foster father to
Ikemefuna for three years. It is then proper that if Ikemefuna

were to be taken home, Okonkwo should be one of those to accompany him on the journey.

From all this, Okonkwo's decision to follow the elders can be seen to be predicated on role and strategy: as a member of the elders he was supposed to go, and he also had to be there in order to let it seem to Ikemefuna that he was really being taken home. From Okonkwo's later actions when they reached the outskirts of Umuofia, where Ikemefuna would be killed, we can speculate that after Ezeudu's advice, Okonkwo, while leaving with the other elders, was thinking along these lines: "I accept Ezeudu's advice, but since I am one of the elders and since I was the person who went to Mbaino to bring Ikemefuna here and have lived with him for three years, I must accompany the elders in order to create the impression that he is actually being taken home. However, when we reach the place where he is to be killed, I shall withdraw to the rear and let the others kill him."

When they arrive at the place where Ikemefuna is to be killed, what is the turn of events? Again, what options are open to Okonkwo? We have already seen how he withdrew to the rear when they reached Ikemefuna's Golgotha, thereby leaving the others to kill the boy. The events of Ikemefuna's death are described in the following way:

> As the man who had cleared his throat drew up and raised his matchet, Okonkwo looked away. He heard the blow. The pot fell and broke in the sand. He heard Ikemefuna cry, 'My father, they have killed me!' as he ran towards him. Dazed with fear, Okonkwo drew his matchet and cut him down. He was afraid of being thought weak.   (p. 43)

We have already established that the men who returned the following day to take Ikemefuna away are "elders from all the nine villages of Umuofia" (p. 40). Given this fact, we then have at our hands a minimum of nine elders who were to see to the killing of Ikemefuna. When it was time to kill Ikemefuna, the man who we may assume was chosen for the deed either delivered a weak blow or missed his aim entirely. As Ikemefuna "ran towards" (p. 43) Okonkwo for help and protection, none of the other men did anything: neither those immediately behind him nor the two who earlier had gone in front of him. It is clear that Okonkwo was not immediately behind Ikemefuna, for otherwise the author would not have used the phrase "ran towards."

During the brief interval that he was running toward Okonkwo, none of the other elders did anything. They simply failed to do their duty.

When Ikemefuna ran to Okonkwo for protection, what choice had Okonkwo? He could have done any of the following things: (1) give Ikemefuna the desired protection, (2) take him and like Pilate wash his hands of the matter and hand him back to be killed, or (3) kill him himself. The first option is ruled out, as adopting it would have amounted to an open defiance of the Oracle of the Hills and the Caves. It would also have been an affront to all the people of Umuofia. Regarding the second option, one may argue that Okonkwo should have followed the example of Pilate, for this would have been a more humane line of action. Okonkwo's position, however, is quite unlike Pilate's. Pilate was operating within the world of human order. In Okonkwo's case, the oracle had commanded that Ikemefuna should die. Okonkwo was not excluded from bringing about the death of Ikemefuna. It would undoubtedly have been very humane of Okonkwo to behave like Pilate, but the consequence would have been different. To take Ikemefuna and to hand him back to be killed would be as if Okonkwo said to the Oracle of the Hills and the Caves, "I don't dispute what you have said, but I refuse to be the instrument that will bring about what you have decreed." This too would have amounted to a defiance of the oracle. The situation is comparable to that of citizens who feel that a particular law is morally revolting; although they would not prevent others from obeying the law, they themselves would not obey it. We are then left with the third option. Okonkwo killed Ikemefuna.

After Okonkwo had killed Ikemefuna, the authorial voice tells us that Okonkwo's reason for killing Ikemefuna is his fear of being thought weak. The authorial voice is always final, but one doubts whether it is equally always masterful. Okonkwo's killing of Ikemefuna is instinctive. No time was left for him to consider his action. In other words, his killing of Ikemefuna was not premeditated. The immediate circumstances under which he had to kill Ikemefuna seem to have been forced on him by capricious fates. He was not in control of the situation. Rather, the situation was controlling him, and we should not apply the principles of morality to a situation in which he was inexorably led by uncanny fate. Thus far, we can conclude from the evidence before us that by the beginning of the novel, Ikemefuna's

death was already a *fait accompli,* that Okonkwo's action in
killing him is not premeditated, and that the circumstances
which led to his killing of Ikemefuna forced the act on him.

We now turn our attention to our second level of analysis; namely, what critics have made out of the evidence available
in the text. After the killing of Ikemefuna, Okonkwo's closest
friend, Obierika, blames Okonkwo for taking part in the killing
of Ikemefuna.   When Okonkwo accuses him of not coming
along with them when they went to kill Ikemefuna, the following conversation ensues between the two of them:

> 'You know very well, Okonkwo, that I am not afraid of
> blood; and if anyone tells you that I am, he is telling a
> lie. And let me tell you one thing, my friend. If I were
> you I would have stayed at home. What you have done
> will not please the Earth. It is the kind of action for
> which the goddess wipes out whole families.'
> 'The Earth cannot punish me for obeying her mes-
> senger,' Okonkwo said.   'A child's fingers are not
> scalded by a piece of hot yam which its mother puts
> into its palm."
> 'That is true,' Obierika agreed. 'But if the Oracle
> said that my son should be killed I would neither dis-
> pute it nor be the one to do it.'   (pp. 46-47)

Many critics have taken a cue from this and blamed Okonkwo
for killing Ikemefuna. For them, Okonkwo committed an offense by killing Ikemefuna. Okonkwo sees his action differently.
The difference between Okonkwo's view and Obierika's (and by
implication the view of Okonkwo's critics), can be summarized
as the difference between rigid adherence to a sacred order and
the questioning of this sacred order by bringing in considerations
of conventional morality or wisdom. Obierika and Okonkwo's
critics are applying the standards of conventional wisdom to a
situation which entirely transcends it. But for Okonkwo, strict
adherence to the eternal sacred order takes precedence and allows for no human rationalization. Hence he tells Obierika that
the Earth cannot punish him for obeying her messenger.
Obierika concedes this point to Okonkwo. His later statement:
"If the Oracle said that my son should be killed, I would neither
dispute it nor be the one to do it" (p. 47) is then no more than
sheer conventional sentimentality and hypocrisy. Did he not
throw away his own twin children because tradition commanded him to? (p. 87). Of course, the tradition which sees twin
children as abominable does not state that it is the father of the

twin children that must throw them away. Was Obierika not going to take part in razing Okonkwo's house and demolishing
everything there (p. 87)? Here again, custom simply demands
that the house of any person who commits a *female ochu*
("inadvertent murder") should be destroyed. It does not compel
every person to take part in such demolitions. In taking part in
these two activities, Obierika commits the same offense (if offense it may be called) for which he holds Okonkwo guilty.

Furthermore, we need to consider whether a person who
kills a condemned man can be said to have committed an offense and also to consider under what circumstances the person
may or may not be exonerated. The oracle said that Ikemefuna
should be killed. It did not say that Okonkwo should not take
part in carrying out its wish. In the context under consideration,
there is not traditional hangman whose role it is to kill people in
Ikemefuna's predicament. By killing Ikemefuna, therefore,
Okonkwo has not usurped any person's role. He is included in
the possible list of those who can kill Ikemefuna. He kills Ikemefuna. The oracle's wish has been obeyed; by whom is of no
material significance. The application of conventional practical
wisdom to a transcendent, eternal sacred order is again seen to be
inappropriate. We do not apply the same normative rules with
which we deal with ourselves to our dealings with our gods and
ancestors, except where there is no conflict in the application of
such rules to both spheres. And where a conflict exists, the god
take precedence. This is exactly the situation in which Okonkwo
kills Ikemefuna.

Critics are also quick to point out that Okonkwo begins to
suffer many reverses after his killing of Ikemefuna. They see
these reverses as a type of punishment from the gods. Carroll,
Nnolim, and Killam, in the references already cited, appear to
share this view. At this stage it is sufficient to point out that
there is no logical implication between Okonkwo's reversal of
fortunes and his killing of Ikemefuna. They are two different
entities separated in space and time, and no causal link can be established between them. More confounding and illogical is
Oladele Taiwo's claim that

> when one considers the trend of events, and it turns out
> later that it is in the funeral ceremony of Ezeudu (who
> had warned Okonkwo to have no part in Ikemefuna's
> death) that Okonkwo is involved in an accidental
> killing that exiles him from Umuofia, one begins to
> wonder whether Obierika's has not been the voice of

> reason; whether in fact, Okonkwo has not misinter-
> preted the will of the gods. . . . We are confronted with
> an ironic situation in which Okonkwo in his attempt to
> uphold 'the authority and decision of the Oracle' dis-
> pleases the earth goddess.   (p. 119)

The chasing of literary motifs is as interesting as it is complex, but sometimes it backfires. The curious logic which links Okonkwo's subsequent tragedies with the killing of Ikemefuna fails to link the deaths of Ezeudu and his son with his part in warning Okonkwo not to have anything to do with the propriety of his action. If Okonkwo is to be held guilty of any offense, it is not that of killing Ikemefuna (i.e., carrying out the wish of the Oracle of the Hills and the Caves) but that of taking an uncanny pride in his action, thereby removing the act from its proper domain or locale. His offense is that of hubris.

Finally, it can be argued that if Okonkwo had committed an offense by killing Ikemefuna, he would have been reprimanded or punished according to established rules. For an offense like the breaking of the Week of Peace, he was reprimanded. For the involuntary killing of Ezeudu's son, he suffers the appropriate punishment: the demolition of his entire compound and a seven-year exile for him and his entire family. If by traditional ethos, he committed an offense by killing Ikemefuna, then he would have been punished. He is not told to perform any cleansing rites. He is not told to offer sacrifices to the Earth goddess or to any other goddess for that matter. He is not deprived of his exalted position among the elders. Undoubtedly, within the level of private morality, his action is unconscionable without *ipso facto* being offensive, and in the near-fatalistic world view with which we are dealing, we have unconscionable acts that our failure to execute could constitute an offense against the gods. A classic example in African literature is the fate of Shanka in Gabre-Medhin's *Oda-Oak Oracle*. Okonkwo's killing of Ikemefuna is an unconscionable act, but we cannot logically go beyond that to establish that by killing Ikemefuna he committed an offense.

Works Cited

Achebe, Chinua. *Things Fall Apart*. London: Heinemann, 1958, 1965.

Carroll, David. *Chinua Achebe*. New York: Twayne, 1970; London: Macmillan, 1980.

Iyasere, Solomon. "Narrative Technique in *Things Fall Apart*." *Critical Perspectives on Chinua Achebe*. Ed. C. L. Innes and Bernth Lindfors. London: Heinemann, 1978, 92-110.

Killam, G. D. *The Writings of Chinua Achebe*. Rev. ed. London: Heinemann, 1977.

Nnolim, Charles E. "Achebe's *Things Fall Apart*: An Igbo National Epic." *Modern Black Literature*. Ed. S. Okechukwu Mezu. New York: Black Academy, 1977, 56- 60.

Taiwo, Oladele. *Culture and the Nigerian Novel*. London: Macmillan, 1976.

Wren, Robert W. *Achebe's World: The Historical and Culture Contexts of the Novels of Chinua Achebe*. Washington: Three Continents, 1980.

Okonkwo's Participation in the Killing of His "Son" in Chinua Achebe's *Things Fall Apart*: A Study of Ignoble Decisiveness

Solomon O. Iyasere

No episode in Achebe's memorable novel, *Things Fall Apart*,[1] is more shocking and heartrending than the execution of Ikemefuna, an event too dreadful to endure. Circumstances surrounding the event make it even more hideous—if that is possible—and invite our moral revulsion more intensely than the killing of the messenger. Commenting on the significance of the murder of Ikemefuna, David Carroll writes:

> The death of Ikemefuna is a turning point in the novel. The guardianship of the boy was a mark of Okonkwo's hard-won status and the highest point of his rise to power. The execution of Ikemefuna is the beginning of Okonkwo's decline, for it initiates the series of catastrophes which ended in his death. But this event is not only a milestone in the career of the hero. The sympathetic rendering of Ikemefuna's emotions as he is being marched through the forest to his death has wider implications.[2]

As crucial as this episode is to the overall thematic and structural development of the novel, especially in the development of the central character, critics have paid only cursory attention to it. With the exception of a brief study by Damian Opata, most of the comments on the killing of Ikemefuna, particularly those treating Okonkwo's participation, have been superficial and judicial, far less extensive and vigorous than the event demands.

The vexing, and paradoxical, question raised by Ikemefuna's death is why Okonkwo takes part, particularly after Ogbuefi Ezeudu, a respected elder in Umuofia who understands its val-

ues and traditions and the habits of the gods, warns Okonkwo
against participating:

> 'That boy calls you father. Do not bear a hand in
> his death.' Okonkwo was surprised, and was about to
> say some things when the old man continued: 'Yes,
> Umuofia has decided to kill him. The Oracle of the
> Hills and Caves has pronounced it. They will take him
> there. But I want [you] to have nothing to do with it.
> He calls you father.'   (pp. 59-60)

In defense of Okonkwo's participation, Damian Opata argues that Okonkwo has no choice but to comply with the monstrous decree of the gods; further, because Ikemefuna is already
regarded as a sacrificial lamb, his death already a *fait accompli*,
Okonkwo acts only as a messenger executing the decree of the
gods. To stress Okonkwo's place as a victim who deserves our
sympathy instead of our vilification, Opata writes:

> Okonkwo's killing of Ikemefuna is instinctive. No time
> was left for him to consider his actions. In other words,
> his killing of Ikemefuna was not premeditated. The
> immediate circumstances under which he had to kill
> Ikemefuna seem to have been forced on him by capri-
> cious fate, he was not in control of the situation.
> Rather, the situation was controlling him and we
> should not apply the principles of morality to a situa-
> tion in which he was inexorably led by uncanny fate.[3]

The inaccuracies of Opata's view derive from his unin-
formed reading of the text; Opata disregards the particularities of
the rhetoric of Achebe's controlled presentation of Okonkwo's
actions throughout the novel and of the circumstances leading
to his execution of Ikemefuna. For example, nowhere in the
novel is it hinted that if Okonkwo had time to reflect on the execution he would have acted differently, as Opata seems to imply.
In fact, a close reading of the text shows that Okonkwo was informed of the intended execution by Oguefi Ezeudu two full days
before the execution was carried out (pp. 59-60); if Okonkwo had
been a man of thought and not of blind action, he would have
reflected on the moral consequences of his action during those
two days. To demonstrate his eagerness to participate in the execution, "Okonkwo got ready quickly [when] the party set out
with Ikemefuna carrying a pot of wine" (p. 60).

To suggest, as Opata does, that Okonkwo is a victim of
fate, one forced by circumstances beyond his control to kill Ikemefuna, is inaccurate. Although the capricious gods decreed

that the innocent Ikemefuna should be killed, the gods did not specifically order Okonkwo to participate in the event. The fact is that Okonkwo was free to choose not to participate in Ikemefuna's execution, as the following conversation between Okonkwo and his friend Obierika makes plain:

> 'I cannot understand why you refused to come with us to kill that boy,' he [Okonkwo] asked Obierika.
> 'Because I did not want to,' Obierika replied sharply. 'I had something better to do.'
> 'You sounded as if you question the authority and the decision of the Oracle, who said he should die.'
> 'I do not. Why should I? But the Oracle did not ask me to carry out its decision.'
> 'But someone had to do it. If we were all afraid of blood, it would not be done. And what do you think the Oracle would do then?'
> 'The Earth cannot punish me for obeying her messenger,' Okonkwo said. 'A child's fingers are not scalded by a piece of hot yam which its mother puts into its palm.'
> 'That is true,' Obierika agreed. 'But if the Oracle said that my son should be killed, I would neither dispute it nor be the one to do it.'   (p. 69)

Opata's argument that Okonkwo is a victim of fate denies him his tragic stature and thereby robs him of our deepest sympathy.

More responsive to Ikemefuna's execution and Okonkwo's role in it is David Carroll, who writes:

> This incident is not only a comment on Okonkwo's heartlessness. It criticizes implicitly the laws he is too literally implementing. . . . As we watch him [Ikemefuna] being taken unsuspectingly on his apparently innocent journey, the whole tribe and its values is [sic] being judged and found wanting. For the first time in the novel, we occupy the point of view of an outsider, a victim, and from this position the community appears cruel.[4]

Carroll's comment is to the point in directing our attention to Okonkwo's heartlessness and his literal minded acceptance of the decree of the gods. However, it does not specifically address the crucial question of whether or not Okonkwo had the choice of refusing to participate in the gods' hideous decree nor why Okonkwo interprets the gods so literally.

Okonkwo was faced with a paradoxical situation in participating in Ikemefuna's death. On the one hand, his relationship with the boy had evolved into a strong paternal/filial relationship; on the other hand, the gods decreed that the boy must die—a decree which had to be obeyed without question—as did the decree that the twins must die, as Obeirika recalled:

> [W]hat crime had they committed? The Earth had de-
> creed that they were an offense on the land and must be
> destroyed. And if the clan did not exact punishment for
> an offense against the goddess, her wrath was loosed on
> the land and not just the offender. As the elders saw, if
> one finger brought oil, it soils the others.   (p. 130)

The important question raised here is why does Okonkwo participate in executing Ikemefuna? Does he fear and respect the wrath of the gods? Judging from Okonkwo's actions, we have to say that the answer is "no"; habitually, Okonkwo acts too impulsively, too violently, to think of the consequences of his actions. This habit of impulse is made clear, for example, when Okonkwo beats his wife during the sacred Week of Peace—a week of harmony, restraint, and decorum: "And when she returned, he beat her heavily. In his anger he had forgotten that it was the Week of Peace. His first two wives ran out in great alarm, pleading with him that it was the sacred week. But Okonkwo was not the man to stop beating somebody half-way through, not even for fear of a goddess" (p. 31). In fact, because of his excessive pride, because he would not admit his error, "people said he had no respect for the gods" (p. 32). Though not afraid of a goddess, Okonkwo is not fearless, for he fears failure, as the narrator tells us:

> [H]is whole life was dominated by fear, the fear of
> failure and of weakness. It was deeper and more inti-
> mate than the fear of evil and capricious gods and of
> magic. . . . Okonkwo's fear was greater than these. It
> was not external but lay deep within himself. It was
> the fear of himself, lest he should be found to resemble
> his father.   (p. 140)

Robert Wren emphasizes Okonkwo's freedom to choose not to participate in killing Ikemefuna, "[I]f a man says 'no' strongly enough, his 'chi' says 'no' also. Okonkwo had that within him which said 'no' to the killing of Ikemefuna."[5]

Does he act, then out of his own selfish motives—his in-ordinate ambition to be acknowledged as one of the courageous and brave men of Umuofia? Does he perceive the decree of the gods as a challenge to his manhood and, as a result, exceeds in his actions even what the gods demand? Based on a careful analysis of Achebe's controlled presentation of Okonkwo's character, his habit of mind and action, as this paper contends, Okonkwo's participation results not from obedience to the gods. Instead, like Ezeulu in *Arrow of God*, Okonkwo is in competition with the gods and acts out of his pathological fear of being thought weak—his fear of being perceived as like his father Unoka.

Because of the centrality of the scene in which Ikemefuna is killed to our understanding of Okonkwo's role in it, it is necessary to cite the passage of length:

> At the beginning of their journey the men of Umuofia talked and laughed about the locust, about their women, and about some effeminate men who had refused to come with them. But as they drew near to the outskirts of Umuofia, silence fell upon them too.
>
> The sun rose slowly to the center of the sky, and the dry, sandy footway began to throw up the heat that lay buried in it. Some birds chirruped in the forest around. The men trod dry leaves on the sand. All was silent. Then from the distance came the faint beating of the ekwe. . . .
>
> They argued for a short while and fell into silence again, and the elusive dance rose and fell with the wind. Somewhere a man was taking one of the titles of the clan, with music and dancing and a great feast. . . .
>
> Thus the men of Umuofia pursued their way, armed with sheathed machetes, and Ikemefuna, carrying a pot of palm wine on his head, walked in their midst. Although he had felt uneasy at first he was not afraid now. Okonkwo walked behind him. He could hardly imagine that Okonkwo was not his real father. He had never been fond of his real father, and at the end of three years he had become very distant indeed. . . .
>
> As the man who had cleared his throat drew up and raised his machete, Okonkwo looked away. He heard the blow. The pot fell and broke in the sand. He heard Ikemefuna cry, 'My father, they have killed me!' as he ran towards him. Dazed with fear, Okonkwo drew his machete and cut him down.
>
> (pp. 61-63)

This tragic event takes place during or immediately after the celebration of the coming of the locust—an occasion of joy, laughter, and excitement, especially among the children of Umuofia. "Locusts are descending" was joyfully chanted everywhere, and men, women, and children left their work or their play to run into the open to see the unfamiliar sight. Ikemefuna's death comes only two days after "Okonkwo sat in his obi

cruching happily with Ikemefuna and Nwoye and drinking
palm wine copiously . . ." (p. 59), sharing with Ikemefuna the joy
which enveloped the whole community. The feast of the locust
thus serves as a foil for and throws into sharp relief the killing of
Ikemefuna.

These contrasting events are presented as occurring almost simultaneously to underscore the paradoxical nature of the
Umuofia society. On the very day that Ikemefuna sits happily
with his "father" Okonkwo, Ezeulu reports, "Yes, Umuofia has
decided to kill him" (p. 59). The narrator's terse, mournful
description of Ikemefuna's death intensifies both the horror of
the event and the dastardliness of Okonkwo's participation: His
"son" runs to him for protection only to be felled by the hard
steel of Okonkwo's machete. Okonkwo's deliberate participation
makes the death of Ikemefuna too horrible to endure.

Okonkwo is consistently presented in the novel, as in the
above episode, as a man of ignoble decisiveness, one who acts
strong but is mentally weak. He is a man who rushes headlong
into action and will not allow himself to be constrained, as he
should be, by the bonds of interpersonal relationships, by
the prickings of conscience, or by the customs and values of his
society.

Okonkwo's predisposition to commit himself with tragic
intensity to irrevocable violence is made clear in the narrator's
first description of him:

> He was tall and huge and his bushy eyebrows and wide
> nose gave him a severe look. He breathed heavily, and
> it was said that when he slept, his wives and children
> in their houses could hear him breathe. When he
> walked, his heels hardly touched the ground and he
> seemed to walk on springs, as if he was going to pounce
> on somebody. And he did pounce on people quite often.
> He had a slight stammer and whenever he was angry
> and could not get the words out quickly enough, he
> would use his fists. . . .   (p. 4)

Emphasis here and throughout is on Okonkwo's intimi-
dating physical strength and his reliance on force to achieve his
ends. As Eustace Palmer observes, "In a sense, Okonkwo is presented as a life-denying force. He was always associated with
death, whereas his father, with all his faults is associated with
life . . . always charged and tense like a loaded cannon. . . . [O]ne
expects his fiery temper and nervous energy to find outlet in violent action in that he will plunge headlong into self destruc-

tion."[6]   Equally important, the narrator's emphasis on Okonkwo's monstrous energy and brute strength calls attention to Okonkwo's primary weakness—his inability to think, to use language to channel and communicate his thoughts and thereby interact meaningfully with his environment.

To Okonkwo, words are mere shapes to fill a void, not prime instruments for conceptual expression or for giving outward experience its form and making it definite and clear. According to Susan Langer, "All genuine thinking is symbolic, and the limits of expressive media are therefore really the limits of our conceptual powers. Beyond these, we have only blind feeling, which records nothing and conveys nothing, but has to be discharged in action . . . or other impulsive demonstrations."[7] Because of his limited metacognitve power, Okonkwo habitually resorts to blind and impulsive actions; he approaches every problem—no matter how complex or paradoxical—with a single-minded, preconceived solution: force without thought, action without regard for consequence. Unlike his friend Obierika, his uncle Uchendu, and his father Unoka, Okonkwo is too impatient, too much a man of action to deal with subtleties, with nuances that do not fit easily into his monochromatic view of life. Okonkwo's rigid use of language corresponds to his rigid approach to life. (In significant ways, his attitude towards life and language help explain why he accepts the decree of the gods literally, without question.) Okonkwo's rhetorical ineptitude further alienates him from Umuofia, further divorces him from his goal of being Umuofia's champion, because Umuofia prides itself on its rhetorical refinement. In Umuofia, as among the Ibos, the art of conversation is regarded highly, and proverbs "are the palm oil with which words are eaten." As Wren observes, Okonkwo "does occasionally use a proverb—four or five times in the course of the novel—but they do not seem to flow from him. . . ."[8] In general, Okonkwo finds words poor substitutes for action. As C. L. Innes observes, "Phrases or statements which reaffirm rather than extend the existing world view of a person or his society are typical of Okonkwo. . . . His contributions to a discussion are generally short and commonplace. . . . For Okonkwo talking is never a prelude to action, it leads nowhere."[9] Lacking rhetorical skill, Okonkwo overcompensates for his deficiency in this area by being too quick to act, by doing more than Umuofia and even the gods demand.

Okonkwo possesses a monumental commitment to placing success and achievement above everything else—even the
need to love and be loved—and identifying his whole existence
with gaining power as one of the lords of the clan of Umuofia.
The commitment to and drive for power rule his life. Worse
still, this habit of mind leads tragically to Okonkwo's denial of
his true self and makes inevitable his suicide. He resorts to force
instead of dialogue, acts violently when flexibility and compassion are called for.

The murder of Ikemefuna, though the most dreadful, is
the climax of a series of extreme actions Okonkwo takes to assert
his manliness—his existence. Other key moments arise when
he savagely beats his son, repudiates his father, Unoka, kills the
messenger, and ultimately turns his own violent hand against
himself.

Okonkwo's impulsive violence marks his relationship
with his only biological son, Nwoye. The boy seeks his father's
love and understanding, but Okonkwo is incapable of responding to these basic human needs; he considers them unmanly and
effeminate. When Okonkwo is confronted by the failure of his
own rigid code as Nwoye turns to Christianity for love and suc-
cor, Okonkwo responds in the only way he knows—with violence:

> It was late afternoon before Nwoye returned. He went
> into the obi and saluted his father, but he did not an-
> swer. Nwoye turned around into the inner compound
> when his father, suddenly overcome with fury, sprang
> to his feet and gripped him by the neck.
>   'Where have you been?' he stammered. Nwoye
> struggled to free himself from the choking grip.
>   'Answer me!' roared Okonkwo, 'before I kill you!'
> He seized a heavy stick that lay on the dwarf wall
> and hit him two or three savage blows.
>   'Answer me!' he roared again. Nwoye stood look-
> ing at him and did not say a word. The women were
> screaming outside, afraid to go in.
>   'Leave that boy at once,' said a voice in the outer
> compound. It was Okonkwo's uncle, Uchendu. 'Are you
> mad?'
>   Okonkwo did not answer. But he let hold of
> Nwoye, who walked away and never returned.
>   (p. 157)

In another crucial event, the final gathering of the clan,
everything seems to point toward the need for dialogue and flex-

ibility in responding to the clan's increasing fragmentation, "They have broken the clan and gone their several ways. . . . Our brothers have deserted us and joined a stranger to soil their fatherland. If we fight the stranger we shall hit our brothers and perhaps shed the blood of a clansman" (p. 210). Okonkwo reacts predictably, decisively, violently. Early in the morning, under a somber silence, the elders of Umuofia gather in the marketplace to decide collectively what action they will need to take to stop the Reverend Smith's and the District Commissioner's ruthless violations of the customs and traditions of Umuofia. A foreign judicial system has been established in place of indigenous laws; a foreign religion, Christianity, has begun to supplant the local gods. Umuofia's existence and all that gave the people's lives substance and meaning are being destroyed from within and without. As the elders deliberate, five messengers from the District Commissioner arrive, and tragic drama unfolds, with Okonkwo at center stage:

> He [Okonkwo] sprang to his feet as soon as he saw who it was. He confronted the head messenger, trembling with hate, unable to utter a word. The man was fearless and stood his ground, his four men lined up behind him.
>
> In that brief moment the world seemed to stand still, waiting. There was utter silence. The men of Umuofia were merged into the mute backcloth of trees and giant creepers, waiting.
>
> The spell was broken by the head messenger. 'Let me pass!' he ordered.
>
> 'What do you want here?'
>
> 'The white men whose power you know too well have ordered this meeting to stop.'
>
> In a flash Okonkwo drew his machete. The messenger crouched to avoid the blow. It was useless. Okonkwo's machete descended twice and the man's head lay beside his uniformed body.
>
> Okonkwo stood looking at the dead man. He knew that Umuofia would not go to war. He knew because they had let the other messengers escape. They had broken into tumult instead of action. He discerned fright in that tumult. He heard voices asking: 'Why did he do it?'
>
> He wiped his machete on the sand and went away.
>
> (pp. 210-211)

To understand the reason why Okonkwo acts as he does, we need to examine Okonkwo's relationship with Unoka.

Okonkwo's relationship with his father, Unoka, is devoid of love and marked by hate. Okonkwo violently and decisively repudiates Unoka, obliterating his father's existence from his mind because Unoka is known to be weak, a failure: "[H]e had long ago learned how to slay that ghost. Whenever the thought of his father's weakness and failure troubled him, he expelled it by thinking about his own strength and success" (pp. 68-69). At his death, Unoka had no title; when he died, he was not accorded the proper traditional funeral but was buried like a dog. In trying to obliterate all Unoka represents, Okonkwo casts off not only Unoka's undignified irresponsibility but also those positive attributes—love, compassion, creativity—which Unoka embodies. What Okonkwo does not recognize is that by attempting to obliterate his father's reality, he symbolically destroys his own existence and his own place in Umuofia society and ends up, in death, just like his father. To Umuofia, Okonkwo's death by hanging is an abomination, an offense against the earth; as a result, Umuofia buries Okonkwo, as Obierika mournfully observes, "like a dog." The clan's attitude toward Okonkwo's death is tersely summarized: "His body is evil, and only strangers may touch it. . . . We cannot bury him. Only strangers can. We shall pay you men to do it. When he has been buried we will do our duty. We shall make sacrifices to cleanse this deserted land" (p. 214).

Okonkwo's fatal gift is his predisposition to violence; he commits himself with tragic intensity to become the champion of the heroic tradition of Umuofia through extreme and decisive action. These attributes appear to serve him well, especially when he channels his strength towards industry. He throws himself into whatever he does like a man possessed. For example, during the planting season, Okonkwo works daily from cock-crow until the chickens went to roost. He is very strong and rarely became fatigued. Consequently, Okonkwo becomes prosperous and well known throughout the nine villages and beyond; he has a large compound enclosed by a thick wall of red earth, and his own hut, or obi, stands immediately behind the only gate in the wall. Each of his three wives has her own hut and "the barn was built against one end of the red wall and long stacks of red yam stood out prosperously in it" (p. 15). Okonkwo is respected for rising so suddenly from great poverty and misfortune to be one of the lords of the clan.

Paradoxically, the same qualities that contribute to Okonkwo's greatness also account for his isolation, his blindness, and his ruin. To achieve success, fame, and power, Okonkwo habitually resorts to and comes to rely on thoughtless violence. Without regard for consequences, Okonkwo acts: he kills Ikemefuna, beats his son, repudiates his father, butchers the messenger. He becomes the apotheosis of violent action and as such ultimately destroys himself.

Yet Okonkwo is not a classical Machiavellian. Although bound to violence to achieve his goals, deep down in his heart, he is not an evil, heartless man. As I have argued elsewhere,[10] he is capable of love, warmth, and compassion. To maintain the image of his "grandiose self," he struggles and succeeds in burying these positive human attributes within himself because he considers them unmanly. He allows his buried humanity to surface only in private, unguarded moments: for example, it is in the dark that he shows his spontaneous response and deep-felt anguish in saving his dying daughter Ezinma from Chielo, and it is in his private, dark room that he shows *brief* remorse after his brutal killing of Ikemefuna.

On one hand, we admire Okonkwo's heroic determination to achieve personal success and applaud his strong commitment, though futile, to preserve the legacy of Umuofia's heroic tradition. At the same time, we condemn and despise him when his determination to succeed and his commitment to preserve the tradition become an insane preoccupation leading to inhuman acts and violence, such as his slaughtering his "son" Ikemefuna.

All in all, Okonkwo is a man of uncommon achievement and uncommon failure. The overriding paradox of his life and death is that if he had not been obsessed with avoiding the life of failure which his father Unoka lived, he would have been less prone to violence, but if he had been less violent, he probably would not have achieved success as a lord in Umuofia. He is, as tragic heroes often are, a victim of the defects of his virtues.

Notes

[1] Chinua Achebe, *Things Fall Apart* (New York: Astor, 1959). All subsequent quotations from the text are from this edition.

[2] David Carroll, *Chinua Achebe* (New York: Twayne, 1970), pp. 48-49.

[3] Damian Opata, "Eternal Sacred Order Versus Conventional Wisdom: A Consideration of Moral Culpability in the Killing of Ikemefuna in *Things Fall Apart*," *Research in African Literature* 18, 1 (1987), 75-76.

[4] Carroll, p. 49.

[5] Robert Wren, *Achebe's World* (Washington, D.C.: Three Continents Press, 1980), p. 44.

[6] Eustace Palmer, *An Introduction to the African Novel* (London: Heinemann Educational Books, 1972), p. 54.

[7] Susan Langer, *Philosophy in a New Key*, 3rd ed. (Cambridge Harvard University Press, 1987), p. 87.

[8] Wren, p. 57.

[9] C. L. Innes, "Poetry and Doctrine in *Things Fall Apart*," in *Critical Perspectives on Chinua Achebe*, ed. C. L. Innes and Bernth Lindfors (Washington, D.C.: Three Continents Press, 1978), pp. 114, 120.

[10] Solomon O. Iyasere, "Narrative Techniques in *Things Fall Apart*," *New Letters* 40, 3 (1974), 73-93.

Index to Selected Proverbs in
Things Fall Apart

Proverbs are the horses of discourse; when communication is
lost proverbs retrieve it.[1]
(Yoruba)

The concentration of meaning and evocative power of proverbs impart a poetic quality to Achebe's prose. . . . Proverbs do not merely convey a quaint charm, nor are the only part of the elaborate conventions of Ibo society, they have a very important role to play in conversion and are an indispensable aspect of Achebe's style.[2]

(1) Whenever he saw a dead man's mouth he saw the folly of not eating what one had in one's lifetime.[3] Page 3

(2) He who brings Kola brings life. Page 6

(3) Among the Ibo the act of conversation is regarded very highly, and proverbs are the palm oil with which words are eaten. Page 7

(4) Our elders say that the sun will shine on those who stand before it, before it shines on those who kneel under them. Page 8

(5) Among these people, a man was judged according to his worth and not according to the worth of his father. Page 8

(6) Age was respected among his people, but achievement was revered. Page 9

(7) If a child washed his hands, he could eat with Kings. Page 9

(8) When the moon is shining the cripple becomes hungry for a walk. Page 11

(9) When a man is at peace with his gods and his ancestors, his harvest will be good or bad according to the strength of his arm. Page 19

(10) Let the kite perch and let the egret perch, too. If one says no to the other, let his wing break. Page 20

(11) A man who pays respect to the great paves the way for his own greatness. Page 20

(12) A toad does not run in the daytime for nothing. Page 22

(13) An old woman is always uneasy when dry bones are mentioned in a proverb. Page 22

(14) The lizard that jumped from the high iroko tree to the ground said he would praise himself if no one else did. Page 23

(15) Eneke the bird says that "Since men have learned to shoot without missing, he has learned to fly without perching." Page 23

(16) You can tell a ripe corn by its look. Page 23

(17) Looking at a king's mouth, one would think he never sucked at his mother's breast. Page 27

(18) Those whose palm kernels were cracked for them by a benevolent spirit should not forget to be humble. Page 28

(19) When a man says yes, his chi says yes also. Page 28

(20) The little bird nza who so far forgot himself after a heavy meal that he challenged his chi. Page 32

(21) I cannot yet find a mouth with which to tell the story. Page 50

(22) Where are the young suckers that will grow when the old banana tree dies? Page 68

(23) A chick that will grow into a cock can be spotted the very day it hatches. Page 68

(24) A child's fingers are not scalded by a piece of hot yam which its mother puts into its palm. Page 69

(25) When mother cow is chewing grass its young ones watch its mouth. Page 73

(26) If I fall down for you and you fall down for me, it is a play. Marriage should be a play and not a fight; so we are falling down again. Page 75

(27) If one finger brought oil it soiled the others. Page 130

(28) A man cannot rise beyond the destiny of his chi. Page 135

(29) Mother is supreme. Page 138

(30) For whom it is well, for whom is it well? There is no one for whom it is well. Page 139

(31) Never kill a man who says nothing. Page 144

(32) There is something to fear from someone who shouts. Page 145

(33) There is no story that is not true. Page 145

(34) The world has no end, and what is good among one people is an abomination with others. Page 145

(35) I cannot live on the bank of a river and wash my hands with spittle. Page 171

(36) A child cannot pay for its mother's milk. Page 172

(37) The clan was like a lizard; if it lost its tail it soon grew another. Page 177

(38) There was a saying in Umuofia that as a man danced so the drums were beaten for him. Page 191

(39) Whenever you see a toad jumping in broad daylight, then know that something is after its life. Page 209

Notes

[1] Oyekan Owomoyela, *African Literature: An Introduction.* Massachusetts: Crossroads Press, 1979, p. 17.

[2] Eustace Palmer, *An Introduction to the African Novel.* London: Heinemann, 1972, p. 62.

[3] Chinua Achebe, *Things Fall Apart.* New York: Astor-Honor, Inc., 1959, p. 4. All other citations are from this edition.

Selected Bibliography

Ackley, Donald G. "The Male-Female Motif in *Things Fall Apart.*" *Studies in Black Literature* 5.1 (1974): 1-6.

Adebayo, Tunji. "The Writer and the West African Present: Achebe's Crusade Against Cyncisim and Apathy." *African Association of the West Indies Bulletin* 7 (1974): 3-16.

—. "The Past and the Present in Chinua Achebe's Novels." *Ife African Studies* 1.1 (1974): 66-84.

Aji, A. "Ezinma, the Ogbanje Child in Achebe's *Things Fall Apart.*" *College Literature* 20 (1993): 170-175.

Angogo, R. "Achebe and the English Language." *Busara* 7.2 (1975): 1-14.

Asobele, Timothy. "Culture nigeriane, ecriture francaise: *Things Fall Apart* de l'anglais en francais." *International Journal of Translation* 2.2 (1990: 61-72.

Bascom, Tim. "The Black African and the White Man's God in *Things Fall Apart*: Cultural Repression or Liberation?" *Commonwealth Essays and Studies* 11.1 (1988): 70-76.

Boafo, Y. S. Kantanka. "Okonkwo or the Triumph of Masculinity a Determinant of the *Fall of a Hero.*" *Asemka* 1.1 (1974): 7-15.

Bonetti, Kay. "An Interview with Chinua Achebe." *The Missouri Review* 12.1 (1989): 62-83.

Bottcher, Karl H. "The Narrative Technique in Achebe's Novels." *Journal of the New African Literature and the Arts* 13.14 (1972): 1-12

Bowker, Veronisa. "Textuality and Worldliness: Crossing the Boundaries: A Post-Modernist Reading of Achebe, Conrad and Lessing." *Journal of Literary Studies Tydskrift Vir Literaturwetenskap* 5.1 (1989): 55-67.

Brown, Lloyd W. "Cultural Norms and Modes of Perception in Achebe's Fiction." *Research in African Literatures* 3 (1972): 21-35.

Brown, Raymond. "Aspects of *Things Fall Apart.*" *Mambo Review of Contemporary African Literature* 1 (1974): 11-13.

Cairns, P. "Style, Structure and the Status of Language in Achebe, Chinua *Things Fall Apart* and *Arrow of God.*" *World Literature Written in English* 25 (1985): 1-9.

Carroll, David. *Chinua Achebe.* New York: Twayne, 1970.

Champion, Ernest A. "The Story of a Man and His People: Chinua Achebe's *Things Fall Apart.*" *Negro American Literature Forum* 8 (1974): 272-277.

Cobham, Rhonda. "Problems of Gender and History in Teaching of *Things Fall Apart*." *Matatu: Journal of African Culture and Society* 7 (1990): 25-39.

Coulibaly, Yedieti E. "Weeping Gods: A Study of Cultural Disintegration in James Baldwin's *Go Tell It on the Mountain* and Chinua Achebe's *Things Fall Apart*." *Annales de l'Universite d'Abidjan* 9D (1976): 531-542.

Coulon, V. "Achebe, Chinua *Things Fall Apart*." *Research in African Literatures* 13 (1982): 83-84.

Davis, Geoffrey V. and Hena Maes-Jelinek, eds. *Crisis and Creativity in the New Literatures in English: Cross/Cultures.* Amsterdam: Rodopi, 1990.

Devi, N. Rama. "Pre and Post Colonial Society in Achebe's Novels." Rao, 79-86.

Djangone-Bi, N'guessan. "Obi Okonkwo a l'intellectuel desempare." *Annales de l'Universite d'Abidjan* 8D (1975): 229-245.

Ebeogu, Afam. "Igbo Sense of Tragedy: A Thematic Feature of the Achebe School." *Literary Half-Yearly* 24.1 (1983): 69-86.

Egudu, R. N. "Achebe and the Ibgo Narrative Tradition." *Research in African Literatures* 12.1 (Spring 1981): 43-54.

Eko, Ebele. "Chinua Achebe and His Critics: Reception of His Novels in English and American Reviews." *Studies in Black Literature* 6.3 (1975): 14-20.

Ekwem, B. C. "The Offended 'Chi' in Achebe's Novels—A Reply." *Horizon* 3.3 (1965): 34-36.

Emenyonu, Ernest. "Chinua Achebe's *Things Fall Apart*: A Classical Study in Colonial Diplomatic Tactlessness." Peterson, 165.

Fido, Elaine. "Time and Colonial History in *Things Fall Apart* and *Arrow of God*." *Literary Half-Yearly* 21.1 (1980): 64-76

Fraser, R. "A Note on Okonkwo's Suicide." *Obsidian II: Black Literature in Review* 6 (1981): 33-37.

Gere, Anne Ruggles. "An Approach to Achebe's Fiction." *African Quarterly* 16.2 (1976): 27-35.

Glenn, Ian. "Heroic Failure in the Novels of Achebe." *English in Africa* 2.1 (1985): 11-27.

Gowa, H. H. Anniah. "The Novels of Chinua Achebe." *Literary Half-Yearly* 14.2 (1973): 3-9.

Granqvist, R. "The Early Swedish Review of Achebe, Chinua *Things Fall Apart and a Man of the People*." Research in African Literatures 15 (1984): 394-404.

Griffiths Gareth. "Languages and Action in the Novels of Chinua Achebe." *African Literature Today* 5 (1971): 88-105.

Groga-Bada, Emmanuel. "Okonkwo ou la volonte d'un destin exemplaire." *Annales de l'Universite d'Abidjan* 9D (1976): 521-530.

Heywood, Christopher. "Surface and Symbol in *Things Fall Apart*." *Journal of the Nigerian English Studies Association* 2 (1967): 41-45.

Ike, Rosaline. "Tragedy and Social Purpose: The Novels of Chinua Achebe." *Something* 5 (1966): 3-13.

Innes, C. L. and Bernth Lindfors, eds. *Critical Perspectives on Chinua Achebe.* Washington: Three Continents Press, 1978.

Irele, Abiola. "The Tragic Conflict in Achebe's Novels." *Black Orpheus* 17 (1965): 24-32: Rpt. in *Introduction of African Literature: An Anthology of Critical Writing from Black Orpehus.* Ed. Ulli Beier. Evanston: Northwestern University Press, 1967, pp. 167-178.

Iyasere, Solomon O. "Narrative Techniques in *Things Fall Apart.*" *New Letters* 40.3 (1974): 73-93.

—. "Okonkwo's Participation in the Killing of His 'Son' in Chinua Achebe's *Things Fall Apart*: A Study of Ignoble Decisiveness." *CLA Journal* 35.3 (1992): 303-315; also in *English Studies in Africa* 33 (1990): 131-140.

Jabbi, Bu-Buakei. "Fire and Transition in *Things Fall Apart.*" *Obsidian II: Black Literature in Review* 1.3 (1975): 22-36; *Sheffield Papers on Literature and Society* 1 (1976): 64-84.

Janmohamed, A. "Sophisticated Primitivism: The Syncretism of Oral and Literate Modes in Achebe, Chinua *Things Fall Apart.*" *Ariel: A Review of International English Literature* 15 (1984): 19-39.

Jeyifo, Biodun. "Okonkwo and His Mother: *Things Fall Apart* and Issues of Gender in the Constitution of African Postcolonial Discourse." *Callaloo: A Journal of African-American and African Arts and Letters* 16.4 (1993): 847-858.

—. "For Chinua Achebe: The Resilience and the Predicament of Obierika." Peterson, 51-70.

John, Elerius E. "Chinua Achebe: *Things Fall Apart.*" *Recherche, Pedagogie et Culture* 33 (1978): 50-52.

Johnson, John W. "Folklore in Achebe's Novels." *New Letters* 40.3 (1974): 95-107.

Jones, Eldred. "Language and Theme in *Things Fall Apart.*" *Review of English Literature* 5.4 (1964): 39-43.

Killam, G. D. *The Novels of Chinua Achebe.* New York: Africana Publishing Corp., 1969.

Kilma, Vladimir. "Chinua Achebe's Novels." *Philogica Pragensia* 12 (1969): 32-34.

King, Bruce, ed. *Introduction of Nigerian Literature.* New York: Africana Publishing Corp., 1971.

Kirpal, Viney. "*Things Fall Apart*: A Colonial Novel." *The Literary Endeavour: A Quarterly Devoted to English Studies* 4.1-2 (1982): 33-38.

Kortenaar, N. "How the Center is Made to Hold in *Things Fall Apart.*" *English Studies in Canada* 17 (1991): 319-336.

Landrum, Roger. "Chinua Achebe and the Aristotelian Concept of Tragedy." *Black Academy Review* 1.1 (1970): 22-30.

Larson, Charles R. "The Film Version of Achebe's *Things Fall Apart.*" *Africana Journal: A Bibliogrpahic Library Journal and Review Quarterly* 13.1-4 (1982): 104-110.

Last, Brian W. "Literary Reactions to Colonialism: A Comparative Study of Joyce, Cary, Chinua Achebe and John Updike." *World Literature Written in English* 22.2 (1983): 151-170.

Leach, Josephine. "A Study of Chinua Achebe's *Things Fall Apart* in Mid America." *English Journal* 60 (1971): 1052-1056.

Leslie, Omalara. "Chinua Achebe: His Vision and His Craft." *Black Orpehus* 2.7 (1972): 34-41.

Lindfors, Bernth. "Achebe's African Parable." *Presence Africaine* 66 (1968): 13-36.

—. *Approaches to Teaching Achebe's "Things Fall Apart."* New York: *Modern Language Association of America*, 1991.

—. "The Palm Oil with Which Achebe's Words Are Eaten." *African Literature Today* 1 (1968): 3-18: Rpt. in *Folklore* in *Nigerian Literature*. New York: Africana Publishing Co., 1973, pp. 73-93.

Lindfors, Bernth and Ulla Schild, eds. *Neo-African Literature and Culture: Essays in Memory of Janheinz Jahn*. Mainzer Afarika-Studien 1. Wiesbaden: B. Heyman, 1976.

Madubuike, Ihechukwu. "Achebe's Ideas on Literature." *Black World* 24.2 (1974); *New Letters* 40.4 (1974): 79-91: Rpt. in *Presence Africaine* 93 (1975): 140-152; *Renaissance* 2 (1975): 14-19.

Maduka, Chidi T. "African Religious Beliefs in Literary Imagination: Ogbanje and Abiku in Chinua Achebe, J. P. Clark and Wole Soyinka." *The Journal of Commonwealth Literature* 22.1 (1987): 17-23.

McCarthy, B. "Rhythm and Narrative Method in Achebe's *Things Fall Apart*." *A Forum on Fiction* 18 (1985): 243-256.

McDaniel, Richard B. "The Python Episodes in Achebe's Novels." *International Fictional Review* 3 (1976): 100-106.

McDougall, Russell. "Okonkwo's Walk: The Choreography of *Things Fall Apart*." *World of Literature in English* 26.1 (1986): 24-33.

Metress, C. "Approaches to Teaching Achebe's *Things Fall Apart*." *International Fiction Review* 19 (1992): 125-127.

Meyers, Jeffrey. "Culture and History in *Things Fall Apart*." *Critique: Studies in Modern Fiction* 11 (1969): 25-32.

Morna, Colleen Lowe. "Chinua Achebe Speaks on the Role of the African Writer." *New-Africa* 242 (1987): 47-48.

Nance, Carolyn. "Cosmology in the Novels of Chinua Achebe." *Conch* 3.2 (1971): 121-136.

Nance, K. "*Things Fall Apart*: Images of Disintegration in Rodoreda, Merece La'Placa Del Diamant." *Hispanofila* 101 (1991): 67-76.

Naumann, Michel. "La Reception Critique de l'oeuvre de Chinua Achebe." *Commonwealth Essays and Studies* 11.1 (1988): 91-99.

Nnolim, Charles E. "Achebe's *Things Fall Apart*: An Igbo National Epic." *Black Academy Review* 2.1-2 (1971): 55-60: Rpt. in *Modern Black Literature*. Ed. S. Okechukwu Mezu. Buffalo, New York: Black Academy Press, 1971.

—. "The Form and Function of the Folk Tradition in Achebe's Novels." *Ariel: A Review of International English Literature* 14.1 (1983): 35-47.

Ntonfo, A. "Les Voices apposees d'Okonkwo et d'Umuofia dans *Things Fall Apart*." *Conjonction* 156 (1983): 79-89.

Nwachukwu-Agbada, J. "A Conversation with Chinua Achebe." *Commonwealth Essays and Studies* 13.1 (1990): 117-124.

—. "An Interview with Chinua Acheve." *Massachusetts Review: A Quarterly of Literature, the Arts and Public Affairs* 28.2 (1987): 273-285.

Nwahunanya, Chinyere. "Social Tragedy in Achebe's Rural Novels: A Contrary View." *Commonwealth Novel in English* 4.1 (1991): 1-13.

Nwoga, Donatus I. "The Chi Offended." *Transition* 15 (1964): 5.

Obiechina, Emmanuel. "Narrative Proverbs in the African Novel." *Oral Tradition* 7.2 (1992): 165.

—. "Structure and Significance in Achebe's *Things Fall Apart*." *English in Africa* 2.2 (1975): 39-44.

Ogbaa, Kalu. "Death in African Literature." *The Example of Chinua Achebe World Literature Written in English* 20.2 (1981): 201-213.

—. "A Cultural Note on Okonkwo's Suicide." *Kunapipi* 3.2 (1982): 126-134.

—. "An Interview with Chinua Achebe." *Research in African Literatures* 12.1 (1981): 1-13.

Ogunsanwo, Olatubosun. "Transcending History: Achebe's Trilogy." *Neohelicon: Acta Comparationis Litterarum Universarum* 142 (1987): 127-137.

Okafor, Clement A. "A Sense of History in the Novels of Chinua Achebe." *Journal of African Studies* 8 (1981): 50-63.

—. "Chinua Achebe: His Novels and the Environment." *College Language Association Journal* 32.4 (1989): 433-442.

Okafor, Raymond N. "Individual and Society in Chinua Achebe's Novels." *Annales de l'Universite d'Abidjan* 5D (1972): 219-243.

Oko, Emelia A. "The Historical Novel of Africa: A Sociological Approach to Achebe's *Things Fall Apart* and *Arrow of God*." *Conch* 6.1-2 (1974): 15-46.

Olagoke, D. Olu. "Varieties in the English of Achebe." *Literary Half-Yearly* 23.2 (1982): 18-37.

Olorounto, Samuel B. "The Notion of Conflict in Chinua Achebe's Novels." *Obsidian II: Black Literature in Review* 1.3 (1986).

Opata, Damian. "Eternal Sacred Order vs. Conventional Wisdom: A Consideration of Moral Culpability in the Killing of Ikemefuna in *Things Fall Apart*." *Research in African Literatures* 18.1 (1987): 71-79.

—. "The Structure of Order and Disorder in *Things Fall Apart*." *Neohelicon: Acta Comparationis Litterarum Universarum* 18.1 (1991): 73-87.

—. "The Sudden End of Alienation: A Reconsideration of Okonkwo's Suicide in Chinua Achebe's *Things Fall Apart*." *Africana Marburgenisa* 22.2 (1989): 24-32.

Osa, Osayinmwense. "The Quitclaim of Okonkwo and Lord Jim." *Creative Forum: A Quarterly Journal of Contemporary Writing* 1.3 (1988): 9-18.

Oyeleye, Lekan. "Transference as a Stylistic Strategy: An Inquiry into the Language of Achebe's *Things Fall Apart* and *No Longer at Ease*." *Odu: A Journal of West African Studies* 32 (1987): 160-169.

Pati, Madhusudan. "*Things Fall Apart*: An Enquiry into Rasa-Configuration." *The Literary Criterion* 26.1 (1991): 40-53.

Peterson, Kirsten Holst and Anna Rutherford, eds. *Chinua Achebe: A Celebration*. Oxford: Heinemann, 1990.

Ponnuthurai, Charles Sarvan. "The Pessimism of Chinua Achebe." *Critique* 5.13 (1975): 95-109.

Povey, John. *The Novels of Chinua Achebe*. King, 97-112.

Priebe, Richard K. "Fate and Divine Justice in *Things Fall Apart*." Lindfors, 159-166.

—. "Teaching *Things Fall Apart* in a Criticism Course." Lindfors, 123-128.

Quayson, A. "Realism, Criticism, and the Disguises of Both: A Reading of *Things Fall Apart* with an Evaluation of the Criticism Relating to It." *Research in African Literatures* 25 (1994): 117-136.

Ramsaran, J. "Achebe, Chinua: *Things Fall Apart.*" K. Turkington,. *Modern Language Review* 75 (1980): 390-391.

Rao, C. R. Visweswra, ed. *Indian Response to African Writing.* New Delhi: Prestige, 1993.

Reddy, K. "*Things Fall Apart* in an Alienated History: An Assessment of Achebe's Fictional Perspectives." *Journal of Literary Studies* 15.2 (1990): 35-46.

Rhoads, Diana-Akers. "Culture in Chinua Achebe's *Things Fall Apart.*" *African Studies Review* (1993): 61-72.

Rice, Michael. "*Things Fall Apart*: A Critical Appreciation." *Crux: A Journal of the Teaching of English* 10.2 (1976): 33-40.

Robertson, P. J. M. "*Things Fall Apart* and *Heart of Darkness*: A Creative Dialog." *International Fiction Review* 7 (180): 106-111.

Sarma, S. "Okonkwo and His Chi: Notes Towards a Mythological Approach to Achebe's Novels." Rao, 66-70. Ed. A. Ramakrishna.

Scheub, Harold. "When a Man Falls Alone." *Presence Africaine* 74 (1970): 61-89.

Seitel, Peter. "Proverbs: A Social Use of Metaphor." *Genre* 2 (1969): 143-161.

Shelton, Austin J. "The Offended Chi in Achebe's Novels." *Transition* 13 (1964): 36-37.

—. "The 'Palm-Oil' of Language: Proverbs in Chinua Achebe's Novels." *Modern Language Quarterly* 30 (1969): 86-111.

Sibley, Francis M. "Tragedy in the Novels of Chinua Achebe." *Southern Humanities Review* 9 (1975): 359-373.

Smith, Angela. "The Mouth with Which to Tell of Their Suffering: The Role of Narrator and Reader in Achebe's *Things Fall Apart.*" *Commonwealth Essays and Studies* 11.1 (1988): 77-90.

Swann, Joseph. "From *Things Fall Apart* to *Anthills of the Savannah*: The Changing Face of History in Chinua Achebe's Novels." Davis, 191-203.

Taylor, Willene. "The Search for Values Theme in Chinua Achebe's Novel *Things Fall Apart*: A Crisis of the Novel." *Griot: Official Journal of the Southern Conference on Afro-American Studies* 2.2 (1983): 17-26.

Turner, Margaret. "Achebe, Hegel and the New Colonialism." Peterson, 51-70.

Udumukwu, Onyemaechi. "The Antinomy of Anti-Colonial Discourse: A Revisionist Marxist Study of Achebe's *Things Fall Apart.*" *Neohelicon: Acta Comparationis Litterarum Universarum* 18.2 (1991): 317-336.

Urs, S. N. Vikramraj. "*Things Fall Apart*: A Novel from the 'Dark' Continent." *Commonwealth Quarterly* New Delhi 1.1 (1976): 28-34.

Waghmare, J. M. "Chinua Achebe's Vision of the Crumbling Past." G. A. Amur, pp. 117-123.

Wasserman, Julian N. "The Sphinx and the Rough Beast: Linguistic Struggle in Chinua Achebe's *Things Fall Apart.*" *Mississippi Folklore Register* 16.2 (1982): 61-70.

Weinstock, Donald and Cathy Ramadan. "Symbolic Structure in *Things Fall Apart.*" *Critique: Studies in Modern Fiction* 11 (1969): 33-41.

Weinstock, Donald J. "The Two Swarms of Locusts: Judgment by Indirection in *Things Fall Apart*." *Studies in Black Literatures* 2.1 (1971): 14-19.

Wren, Robert. "Ozo in Chinua Achebe's Novels: The View from the Past." *Nsukka Studies in African Literature* 3 (1980): 71-80.

Wright, Derek. "Things Standing Together: A Retrospect on *Things Fall Apart*." Peterson, 165.

Wyner, Sylvia. "History, Ideology and the Reinvention of the Past in Achebe's *Things Fall Apart* and Laye's *The Dark Child*." *Minority Voices: An Interdisciplinary Journal of Literature and the Arts* 2.1 (1978): 43-61.

Index